BUCKING

FOLK
TALES

# BUCKINGHAMSHIRE
# FOLK TALES

TERRIE HOWEY

For Michael Ridley.
Your journey was too short but filled with stories.
It was an honour to know you, and your love of literature.
The Shakespeare story is for you.

First published 2019

The History Press
97 St George's Place
Cheltenham, GL50 3QB
www.thehistorypress.co.uk

© Terrie Howey, 2019

The right of Terrie Howey to be identified as the Author
of this work has been asserted in accordance with the
Copyright, Designs and Patents Act 1988.

British Library Cataloguing in Publication Data.
A catalogue record for this book is available from the British Library.

ISBN 978 0 7509 6767 9

Typesetting and origination by The History Press
Printed and bound in Great Britain by TJ International Ltd.

# CONTENTS

# ACKNOWLEDGEMENTS & ILLUSTRATIONS

In the writing of this book, and the fashioning of my livelihood as a storyteller, there are several people who I need to acknowledge. To the mentors who have given their time, energy and expertise to guide me, I thank you one and all: Andrew Charles, Ksenija Horvat, Robert Howat, Janet Dowling, Shonaleigh Cumbers, Taffy Thomas, Mike Wilson, Antonia Liguori, Kevin Cordi, Joseph Sobol, and Kerry Pace. To friends and fellow storytellers who have walked part of the journey with me and whose inspiration has lighted dark times: Debs Williamson, Juliette Diagre, Belinda McKenna, Kristina Gavran, Theresa Wedderburn (and all of the Order of the Teapot), and to my fellow storytellers at Stony Storytellers and Feast of Fools. To my family, who have had to put up with long hours of research and writing, and the evenings and weekends when I'm never around because I'm off performing: Lynda and Richard Howey, Rooh Moore, Boris and Merlin.

I would also like to offer my most grateful thanks to Katherine Soutar for the lovely cover illustration enticing readers to explore this volume of stories.

However, there is one person to whom I owe a great debt of gratitude, because without his persistent optimism in this, my first writing endeavour, I doubt I would have ever completed this book. I thank Stephen Hobbs for ferrying me to archives when I was ill, being my fellow story-hunting super sleuth, and for being a soundboard for stories that I was not so sure about but sensed had a glimmer of something special about them. He also painstakingly read through the various versions, editing out my dyslexic moments to form the book you read today.

Thank you all, you are all heroes in my story.

# FOREWORD

Once upon a time, a storyteller moved to Stony Stratford with a head full of stories (500 and counting) and a heart full of the joys of storytelling. She formed the Stony Storytellers so that folk might learn the basics of storytelling, create their own stories and then share them with others. Terrie Howey (for it was she, known then as Red Phoenix) provided a safe but challenging environment. People dropped in and out of the group; trips were arranged to see other mighty storytellers, and small rooms were booked for us to fill with our own stories. We were invited to attend Red Phoenix storytelling gigs and asked to critique her performance (we knew the mantra: 'What worked well?' 'Even better if?') only to be told 10 miles out that we had each been given 10 minute open mic slots in the first half of the evening! The journey home was filled with euphoria and endless tales of Nasruddin from driver Phoenix.

My favourite monthly pilgrimage was to 'Storytelling at The Feast of Fools' in Northampton, where Red Phoenix was the inaugural headliner. There we were introduced to magnificent professional tellers, and on alternate months we had our storytelling open mic opportunities. Such events send you scurrying to increase your own repertoire and you begin to wonder about the stories in your own neighbourhood; so, when you have the chance of being involved in that quest you reach out and grab it with both hands.

As a professional librarian of thirty years, surely this would be an easy task for me? A few clicks on the Buckinghamshire County Library catalogue and the British Library catalogue would certainly reveal a treasure trove? Amazon came up with *Buckinghamshire Folk Tales* by Terrie Howey (published by the History Press) with an unspecified publication date. It sounded perfect! If only one had a time machine! But alas, there seemed to be nothing. Buckinghamshire was just another of those counties whose rich seam of folk tales went unmined by Victorian folklorists. So, we had to set out and pan for our own nuggets.

The public library, of course, is a wonderful institution packed with staff who love their services and care deeply about their subjects; especially local interest and local history. But nine years of austerity and relentless cuts to local government budgets have savaged these services. These days, professional library staff are an endangered species and their numbers are so diminished that no one has the time to develop the levels of expertise and background knowledge that were taken for granted a decade ago. It's a rare library, for example, that's able to maintain its local cuttings files and you can no longer talk to X, 'Who knows everything about Y,' because they've gone!

So, the short cuts have almost disappeared, and you have to discover the dead ends for yourself. I had thought the stories might want to be found and they might even be labelled, 'A Story', but what we found were fragments: bits from here and there, stories within stories, a vast jigsaw of stories that had been scattered everywhere. But it takes a storyteller to find these precious fragments and it took a Red Phoenix to point out that they were there, and here, and over there; under my nose all the time. And here they are: a wonderful breathing collection of the most glorious stories. A tapestry of stories! Some I can barely recognise from the original two-line reference or that insignificant newspaper cutting. I had seen them as street names or wall plaques, when they were really the cold trails of long-lost stories.

Although these Buckinghamshire folk tales have been collected together, they are each in need of a new hearth: a place where they can thrive and be shared. This is where you come in.

*By Stephen Hobbs, Seventh Bard of Stony Stratford.*

# INTRODUCTION

As a storyteller, I have always believed that stories hold within them truths about who we are as people; and they are much more important than mere entertainments to while away a few hours. However, it should be said that whiling away a few hours with stories is time well spent.

In this collection you will find stories from throughout Buckinghamshire: an ancient county with flowing rivers, Iron Age track ways, Roman roads, and the Chiltern Hills cutting their path across it. Where its woods once hid outlaws and highwaymen and its proximity to London made it popular with royalty, now busy motorways and new towns allow new residents to settle and make the stories of the future. Talking of new towns, I hope you will discover how Milton Keynes, far from being filled with the rhetoric of newness, is also home to many an old tale.

Finding the stories for this collection has been, at times, a difficult task. Being such a big county, one might naturally assume that there would be an abundance of stories to draw from, especially considering its diverse landscape that has inspired awe, romance and heroism over the years. Yet unlike its neighbouring counties, Buckinghamshire did not draw the attention of folklorists who scoured the countryside for fables, fairy and folk tales. Collectors of songs and stories, such as Cecil Sharp, Ruth Tongue, and Katherine Briggs, seemed to bypass this large county, with only three stories apiece directly connected to Buckinghamshire appearing in the well-sourced collections of Tongue (*Forgotten Folktales of the English Counties*) and Briggs (*Dictionary of British Folk-Tales*).

John Houghton's collection of books recounting past events and notable persons were very useful in signposting where stories might lie hidden but, whilst his coverage of the county (and its neighbours) was wide, his descriptions were sensible, brief and omitted the magic and mystery of the stories. So, I turned to the Centre for Buckinghamshire Studies in Aylesbury with its extensive collections and its knowledgeable and supportive staff. It was there, whilst digging through faded old article clippings and books, whose heady aroma held the centuries in their pages, that I unearthed the majority of the treasures reworked in this book.

I am always interested in finding more stories, so if you possess a tale or two from this fair county that is not held within these pages do please get in touch, and you never know – one day there may be enough for an additional collection. I found a great many more stories besides, and then faced the hard task of deciding which to include and which to leave out. I felt a certain responsibility to include as many as possible to address the absence of interest in this county's stories for so long, and to present them for future story-hunters or national collections. It is my hope that, whether you are native to the county or an interested outsider, you will know this enchanting county all the better for knowing its stories.

I have not always lived in Buckinghamshire, and in fact only arrived in the area in 2013. Prior to that I had lived in Edinburgh (where I received the nickname Red Phoenix as a street teller, entertaining the tourists with the dark tales of 'Auld Reekie's' heritage, the name sticking throughout my career), Hampshire, and the back of my van, as I travelled round the country listening to and telling stories. It was thanks to fellow storyteller Shonaleigh Cumbers that I arrived in Milton Keynes, but that, as she would tell you, 'is another story'. When I arrive in a new place as a storyteller it's important to me to find out its stories because this will tell you a lot about what, or maybe even who, a place is.

To those of you reading this who believe that Milton Keynes lacks stories, I shall point out the last section of this collection and ask you to reconsider. I discovered a wealth of stories within the new town and instantly became entranced, and a little confused that others didn't also see them. So, I set about sharing them whenever I could, and this led to various storytelling opportunities, including: as a living history actress at Bletchley Park; as the education officer at the Milton Keynes City Discovery Centre, tasked with telling the story of the area to local schools, colleges and businesses from around the world; and being involved with the Living Archive and its heritage projects.

Stories have been part of my life since before I can remember and were always more than a bedtime activity enjoyed as a child. Being dyslexic, I found stories were the way in which I could frame information and memorise it, so I could avoid reading and writing. As a result, I started storytelling young, without releasing what it was I was doing, holding court at the edge of the playground telling tales in infant school. The wanderlust of stories never left me.

In my undergraduate dissertation I focused on storytelling. However, my road to becoming a storyteller was difficult. There weren't any academic courses when I started, and only a few storytellers ran short courses where it was great to learn and get to know people. I went and sat at the knee of those who inspired me, and little by little I developed my craft. The generosity of those who mentored me ensured that I too wanted to pass stories on and help smooth the way for the storytellers who came after me.

This led me to provide story coaching classes, workshops, apprenticeships, and to visit Canada and the USA as part of a Winston Churchill Fellowship to explore how new and young tellers were supported so that I too could support new and young UK tellers. In my local town of Stony Stratford, I run the Stony Storytellers, a storytelling coaching group for adults. I am the Chair of the Bardic Council of Stony Stratford and each year we welcome in a new Bard (as well as a youth and junior Bard) to become the voice of the people, using the power of words to celebrate our little corner of Buckinghamshire. In the last few years I have been doing a PhD in applied storytelling, looking at its effect on communities, and teaching a storytelling class at Loughborough University. In all these ways I am hoping to make the way for other storytellers easier and increase the understanding of just how important stories are in our everyday life.

Stories can be a tool for learning, for living, for a safe haven to escape to, or a promise of dreams to chase; they can change your mood, your mind, and maybe even change the world (but for more on that you will have to wait until I publish my PhD thesis). We are all storytellers and affect the world around us by the stories we tell of ourselves, others, and the places we inhabit.

Over the years I have lived in numerous places around the UK and even spent periods of time living abroad in Australia, Italy, and Canada. No matter where I have lived, I have always been a storyteller and my way of understanding my new surroundings and finding my way about has been through stories. I believe the folk tales of a place are much more than charming vignettes of a bygone age, but stories that can connect us to both a space and a past, giving us a sense of place and heritage.

Folk tales are the stories of people, everyday people like you and me, whilst the stories that happen to us may one day become the folk tales of the future. It is because of this that folk tales are important to tell, and listen to, and rediscover, since they share the experiences of what is to be human. Telling folk tales can prepare you for an encounter you have never experienced before; they can remind you that other people have shared similar experiences, or they can even help us process an experience that we may find difficult to deal with. In this sense, folk tales are not stale mementos of the nostalgic past, but an important part of our cognitive and emotional development in the quest to become better people. Folk tales of place have yet another role, and this is to give a voice to the places that we live in, to make it a home we can connect to and give us a sense of shared experience within the communities we live in. They also challenge us and help us to re-evaluate our preconceptions, because stories do have a habit of making the ordinary into the extraordinary and making the fantastical familiar.

The oral tradition of storytelling allows the story to evolve and develop to suit the societies and cultures that need them, and by this process remain relevant. It is my firm belief, therefore, that although books and the internet allow us to engage with a wider selection of stories than ever before, I do urge you not to leave tales hidden in the confines of pages, but to tell them over and over until they evolve and change and become your own.

My belief in the power of stories is so strong that in 2016 I began a PhD, researching how stories as a form of heritage and as a method with which to share heritage can build and strengthen a sense of place, especially in the 'new town' residents of Milton Keynes.

Therefore, over the past few years I've been intensively rooting out and discovering stories that connect not only to Milton Keynes but also to the rest of Buckinghamshire. It has been my delight to find stories of witches and highwaymen in an area that is deemed to be too new to have any cultural heritage. Throughout Buckinghamshire I have discovered stories of miraculous trees, moving boulders, ghosts, fairies and dragons. Each of these stories, whether they are about an old village or a new town, tell us something about the area, giving it a voice to speak through the many years and the many generations that have settled and lived here. These stories give a space a personality, and an emotional presence with which we can connect and gain a sense of place for the home we live in, and a sense of ourselves as we too create stories and future heritage.

I hope, in my small way, that this book of folk tales will add to the pantheon of stories that abound in Buckinghamshire; to give those who live here a sense of pride in their area, and for those who don't, an insight into this old county, with its quaint old villages and large new town.

*Terrie Howey*

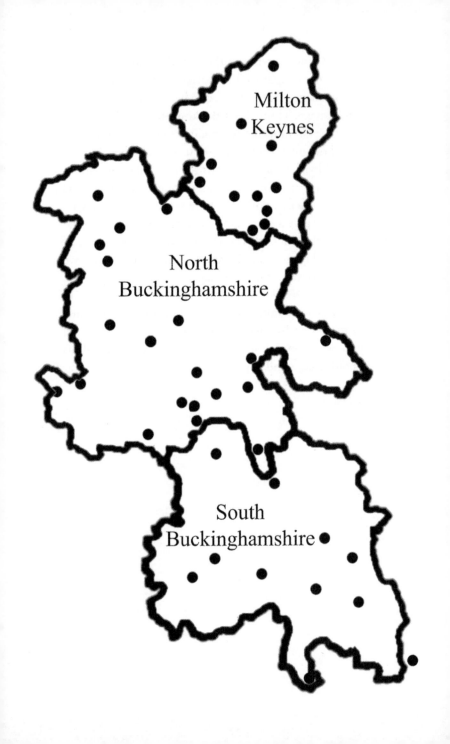

# 1

# STORIES FROM SOUTH BUCKINGHAMSHIRE

## GHOSTIES DON'T LIKE IRON

*This story was collected by Ruth Tongue from a member of the Women's Land Army working in Prestwood in 1938. In days gone by it was a common practice to hammer iron nails into the leather soles of shoes to improve their grip. This gave us the term 'hobnail boot'.*

Once there was a dairymaid called Fat Dolly, a pretty lass who had an eye for the boys. She loved nothing better than to frolic in the hay when she could. Perhaps to curb her licentious ways, she was sent to work on a small farm that had no other maids, so she would be kept busy, and only one farm hand, a lad named Joseph.

Well, as it turns out, busy or not, Dolly's mind soon turned to Joseph, a shy lad a year or so older than herself. She knew that if she were to suggest anything outright poor Joseph would be so abashed, they would get nowhere, so she took to making a plan.

It was that Halloween time of year, when people turn their thoughts to things that go bump in the night, and this gave Dolly an idea.

A night or so after All Hallows' Eve, the evenings were drawing in, and Dolly had rushed to finish her work because she planned to meet up with Joseph just as he was passing the old barn. As he passed her, he saw she was looking nervous and asked what the matter was.

'Oh Joseph, 'tis terrible dark these Halloween nights. I'm frit of ghosties.'

Before the lad knew what was happening, Dolly had clung to him – a feeling that was not so unpleasant. To comfort her, he slid his arm around her, and she nuzzled into him and clung even harder saying she thought she had heard something. This poor damsel in distress started to make Joseph feel most protective and there they stood in the gloom holding one another, with Dolly hiding a sly smile.

'They say a man killed himself up there in the barn. It makes me tremble to think of it, but if we were to go look and find nothing, I am sure I would feel much better.'

Joseph, who now felt quite brave, agreed and they were about to set off on their investigations when the straw rustled and moved. Now truly frightened, for she had managed to scare herself with her own story, Dolly held so tight to Joseph he found it most difficult to breathe. Yet these new feelings of love's ardour stirred in him a latent hero, so wriggling free from her tight grip he pulled off his hobnail boots declaring, 'Ghosties don't like iron and there's plenty in my boots.'

Now frightened out of her wits, Dolly clung on to the brave young lad as Joseph readied himself to launch the boots into the haunted haystack. But with the ample girl cleaving herself, body and soul to him, Joseph's swing went astray and as he launched the boots they flung around and caught the wayward lovers in the head, the left boot for Dolly, and the right for Joseph. The blows knocked the pair flat out, and they collapsed upon the ground.

When all had fallen silent, the old tramp who had nestled himself down in the warm hay for the night crawled out and decided to try the farm further on, for this one was far too noisy.

When the pair recovered, they had a matching set of black eyes, which took some explaining to the farmer and his wife.


## THE VAMPIRE OF BUCKINGHAMSHIRE

*This story was told by Stephen, the Archdeacon of the diocese of Buckinghamshire, to the Augustinian Canon William Parves or William of Newbury as he was known. It is a very unusual story, which takes place in an unnamed place in Buckinghamshire in the year 1192.*

When the man died in the year of our Lord 1192, his wife set about organising a proper funeral for him and for his body to be placed in the family tomb on the eve of the Day of Ascension. All this was done with proper and solemn respect and after the funeral the wife returned home. Following such an emotionally exhausting day, the wife set about her meagre meal and prepared herself for bed. But, in the middle of the night she was awoken as she heard movement in the room. Opening her eyes, she turned to see her husband risen from the grave and back in their bedroom, making his way onto the bed and then pressing his full weight down on top of her as though to crush the life from her and perhaps take it for himself to live once more. She tried to fight him off, but his strength was immense and as the air was being squeezed from her lungs by the pressure of his cold body pressing upon hers, she let out a terrible scream, which seemed to startle the vampire.

So, the woman yelled and screamed further, and the terrible creature left the house and returned unto his grave.

Quite unsure what to do the next night, the woman went to bed with trepidation filling her heart. Again, her husband came creeping in, in the middle of the night, and pressing his terrible weight upon her body. His breath was foul and foetid. She fought and struggled to fend him off to no avail, until like the previous night her screams and yells seem to become too much for the vampire who retreated into the darkness.

The poor woman was now beside herself as to what to do, and so she confided in a few friends, who out of concern or sheer curiosity agreed that they would sit in vigil that night.

And so, as the sun set on the third night after the funeral the woman prepared herself for bed whilst her friends gathered in the corner of the room, silent, watching, waiting. Just like the two previous nights, the husband came again, silent but moving with terrible force onto the bed, onto his wife, pressing down harder and harder. Warned by the wife, the friends knew that the creature seemed to find noise unpleasurable and so they screamed and shouted, fought and kicked until the vampire left that house. However, it seems that whatever dark forces motivated the man to rise from his grave had not been satisfied on that night for he attacked the houses of his brothers who lived on the same street as his wife. There he tormented them in the same manner, trying to press the life out of them. They had heard what they had thought were the wild tales of a grief-stricken wife but, confronted now with the terrible truth, they knew to shout and yell until the creature finally withdrew and the night grew quiet once more.

For nights on end this terrible ordeal continued, first at the wife's house then at the brothers, and when the vampire could find no satisfaction, he started visiting other neighbours in the street until every house had to sit in vigil, night after night, to scare the terrible creature off. Yet still this did not stop the vampire from coming; perhaps he sought to catch people unawares or in a moment of drowsiness, or perhaps it was just his instinct that even he himself could not fight. When he failed to find fulfilment upon the people, he turned his riotous attention to beasts both wild and tame, in field or stable, until they too caused such a ruckus that the vampire had no other course but to return to his tomb.

Soon people were not even safe during the day, for the vampire was now able to walk in daylight. As he wandered the streets, he was seen by only a few; even if groups of people were walking together (as was now their habit) it was not unusual that only one or two would see the terrible creature. To the others he seemed invisible, and yet his presence was felt by all.

With no end in sight to this terrible torment, the people 'alarmed beyond measure', sought the counsel of the Church, appealing to Stephen, the Archdeacon of Buckinghamshire and a gathering of the clergy. 'They detailed the whole affair, with tearful lamentation…' Upon hearing this dreadful story, Stephen wrote a letter to the venerable St Hugh, Bishop of Lincoln, who was residing at the time in London, to tell him of the horrifying things that had been happening in the small Buckinghamshire town.

When the bishop heard the frightful account, he was indeed shocked, and called upon his advisors, the priests and theologians. They alarmed him even more by saying that this was not an isolated event, and that other stories such as this had been heard all over England; in their wisdom and experience, the only way to deal with the creature was to dig up the body and burn the corpse.

Upon hearing this, St Hugh thought that this was an unchristian way to behave: 'indecent and improper to the last degree'. The bishop decided instead that he would write a letter of Absolution of Sin.

Once written, the bishop travelled to the troubled town and insisted that the tomb be opened so that he may inspect the state of the man's body. When the tomb was opened, the cadaver inside showed no signs of decay. The bishop needed no further proof, and so he laid the letter of absolution on the man's chest and commanded that the tomb be closed once more, for now the vampire would not be permitted to inflict any more harm upon the persons of the town. Henceforth the vampire was never seen or heard of again.

## THE POACHER

*During the late 1600–1800s something changed all across England; under the Enclosures, the landlords started putting fences around the borders of their land. These places went from being common land, where people could graze their cattle, go foraging for nuts and mushrooms, or hunt, to being out of bounds. Now, suddenly the poor were restricted as to where they could go, and wealthy landowners employed gamekeepers to keep a tight watch on the plants and animals of their woodlands and meadows. The poor became even poorer because now, if they had no money, they couldn't go out to nature's bounty to fill their larder either. So, the practice of poaching became common amongst those with little means to feed their families.*

The woodlands once covered a much wider area than it does now, and it stretched right across the county. All around, poor folk could see the abundance of food, which they knew they dared not take. It made their bellies ache and their heads throb. And so it was, that two farmworkers, Bill and Nell, faced the winter months with little work to do and food scarce upon the table. They watched each day as their two boys William and Jack grew thinner and the hunger gnawed at their very bones. Bill decided that he was going to do something about it, and the only thing he could think of was a spot of poaching.

So, Bill called up his brother Ned and with some friends they made their plans. Bill decided that his own boys, William (seventeen) and Jack (fourteen), were old enough to join them so that they could learn the ways of the land. It was a cold, crisp evening and the moon was shining bright when they all set off, much to Nell's annoyance because she had heard about the local gamekeeper. So too had Ned, because the gamekeeper was said to be a vicious one, and they would be lucky to get out alive if he caught them. Sometimes when you're hungry you don't think straight, and Ned was already so nervous that they really should never have given him the gun. All Ned wanted to do was bag the first thing he could and then get out of that wretched place before they got caught. He saw that the hill was covered with rabbits; in a moment, Ned had the gun to his shoulder and fired – completely missing.

'What have you done?' hissed Bill. 'That shot will be heard across the woods, and that devil of a gamekeeper will be coming this way.' He was right. The gamekeeper was the other side of the hill; he had heard the shot and began to make his way towards the sound.

Bill and Ned were so busy arguing, the way that only brothers can argue, that they didn't notice the gamekeeper creeping towards them. Even as the keeper was raising his pistol to fire a warning shot so that the poachers would turn around and he could get a good look at their faces in the moonlight, they continued their squabble.

But young Jack saw the moonlight glinting on the gun-metal and dashed forward thinking that someone was going to shoot his father. As he leapt up, the gun fired, young Jack fell to the ground a bloody hole in his chest.

Bill lunged at the gamekeeper, who pushed him away shouting, 'I didn't mean to do it!'

'Da!' cried William. 'We've got to get him help.' So, the unsuccessful poachers grabbed the injured boy and disappeared into the darkness, leaving the gamekeeper to tend his bruises.

Before they were even halfway home, Jack breathed his last, and all they could do was let a grieving mother prepare her youngest son for a cold grave.

Yet before they had time to mourn, Bill, William, Ned and the others were arrested for poaching and put in gaol to await the assizes. Three weeks passed until a makeshift courtroom could be assembled in the back room of a local public house.

The judge sat and listened as the gamekeeper gave his evidence before the local lord of the manor, who nodded solemnly in his finery, whilst the gaunt and sparsely clad poor folk began to mumble. A great cry of 'Injustice!' was called out, and the judge threatened to clear the room when a pale thin hand rose above the crowd. It was Nell. The judge nodded to her to come forward.

'What is it you want to say?'

She stood there looking at her husband and son, and then she spoke: 'It seems to me that often no one speaks on behalf of us poor, and the law most times is against those who need protecting the most. I may not have the knowing of a judge, or the money of a lord, but I am a mother who has just lost her son, and that brings a knowing of another kind. I see there the man who killed my boy, standing free and doing his upmost to bereft me of my other son and husband. Here stands the accused, who to my mind, not having succeeded in taking even a single rabbit, did no further crime than walk in the woods wanting a full belly. Ask yourself why a man would risk so much for so little? We are starving, and if you take my men then I will surely starve and that will also be on your judgement. So, I beg to you, Sir, let my menfolk go. Let my one remaining son come home to me. For if you will not judge a killer, how can you judge a poacher? Let the keeper be judged in heaven for surely he will pay a higher punishment in the end.'

Upon hearing that, the judge acquitted the would-be poachers. Whilst by law the gamekeeper was not tried, for he was protecting his master's lands, he was driven far from that place, and in time he faced the everlasting judgement beyond the grave. And what happened then, who can say? But by Nell's words, I'm sure he paid.

## WITCH'S STONE TREASURE

*On the boundaries of the village of Speen, look carefully in the bushes and you will find two large stones. These are ancient standing stones. Both stones are said to mark a grave containing treasure and haunted by the occupant, but don't go grabbing your spade just yet. The first stone is said to be Nanny Cooper's grave, and the second tucked just behind is cited as John Cooper's grave. Any relationship between these two Coopers was never found, but it more than likely as both were reputed to live in the cottages that stand close to the site of the stones.*

## Nanny Cooper

Once there was a little old woman who lived in one of the tiny cottages on the edge of Speen village. Some say she might've been a witch, others say she was just a little eccentric, but whatever you think, she was a kindly old woman who went about her day helping others. It has been lost to memory exactly why she did her daily routine, but she was often seen going down to the pond where a tall tree grew with branches reaching out over the body of water. Here she would attach a basket by a rope to one of the branches of the tree, clamber inside and swing herself across to the other side of the pond. Maybe this was a quicker route than walking around the pond or she had a rather strange way of fishing, but whatever the reason, one day she clambered into the basket and, as it swung out across the pond, the branch broke. Nanny Cooper and the basket tumbled down into the water, which quickly filled up and began to sink, sucking poor old Nanny Cooper down with it. Her drowned body was recovered and was buried with the large stone placed on top of her, because they say she found treasure in that there pond, which was also placed in her grave with her. But should you go looking for it, her ghost will rise up and stop you!

## The Highwayman

Times were tough for the poor folk of Buckinghamshire; it was hard to know where the next coin was coming from or where to get food to put on the table. Bellies went empty and sleep would not come to those who spent listless nights worrying about their woes. One such poor soul was John Cooper who lived in one of the cottages on the edge of the village of Speen. Can you imagine what it was like for poor folks like John to watch the rich and the wealthy who lived in the large estates and manor house that abound the county;

their fancy carriages rolling past, filled with gentlemen and ladies gilded with silks, gold and precious jewels?

Many a wealthy carriage would frequent the road between Highwood Bottom and Princes Risborough, which came right through Speen, so John would see them every day. Little by little, the annoyance at the injustice ate at John and grew into a large frustration, which grew into an anger, and then into a great rage. It was so unfair that some people had so much while everyone else had so little, and he for one was not going to put up with it anymore.

Saddling up his horse, he placed a pistol in his belt and, tying a mask around his face, John Cooper turned highwayman up and down that road through Speen.

Much to John's fortune, and to the misfortune of the wealthy, it turned out that John Cooper was indeed a very fine highwayman. To the cry of 'Stand and Deliver', he stole coins, gold and silver, precious jewels, strings of pearls, brooches, necklaces, bracelets, earrings, rings – anything, in fact, that wasn't nailed down. By the time he returned to his small cottage in the early morning after a hard night's pillaging, his pockets would be overflowing. In next to no time at all, John Cooper became a wealthy man.

But, alas, such a lifestyle is not a long one, and it wasn't long before the authorities were hot on his trail. He was arrested, tried at the local assizes and found guilty of highway robbery, for which the punishment was death by hanging. John knew that as a criminal he would have no Christian burial in a churchyard, but instead would be buried on unconsecrated ground.

The eve before his execution, he was allowed a visitor, a good and trusted friend. John asked that he be buried at a certain spot near his cottage and that a large stone should be placed over his grave. His friend promised to do just as he asked, and with that John was left to sit alone in the darkness contemplating his last night on this Earth.

The next morning the highwayman John Cooper was taken to the very road upon which he used to rob and there, standing tall on the roadside, was a makeshift gibbet tree from which hung a rope. The rope was placed around his neck and there John Cooper danced the Tyburn jig until his soul passed into the next life.

John's body was left to hang by the side of the road as a warning to other would-be highwaymen. After the allotted time, John's faithful friend came forward to collect the body and, just as John had asked, made sure that he was buried close to his cottage, and a large stone placed over the grave. That should have been the end of this story, but it isn't. You see, no matter how much the authorities searched, they could not find a single piece of the booty John had stolen. It seems he had sold or spent very little of it, so where was it? People searched the cottage, but nothing was found. They questioned friends and neighbours but none of them knew (or if they did, they kept it to themselves). They searched nooks and hollows along the road, and still nothing. It was then that people started to wonder that maybe John had arranged to be buried with his treasure. He was a highwayman after all; perhaps he had taken the treasure, which had cost him his life, to the grave. One or two brave souls decided that they would move that heavy stone, dig up his grave and search for the highwayman's treasure. They waited until the moon was full and set off with pickaxes and shovels in hand.

No sooner had they arrived at the stone than the air filled with a chill that cut to the bone and mist seeped from the ground. The closer they got to the stone, the stranger things became: the sound of a horse braying when no horse was there; the sound of groaning when all present swore it wasn't them. Then, rising slowly out of the grave and stepping over the stone, John Cooper appeared, pistol in hand, saying, 'Stand and Deliver'. This gave such a fright to the men that they ran away home and left the dreams of the highwayman's treasure buried underneath that stone.

It has been said that over the years many other foolish, greedy, desperate individuals have tried to take the highwayman's treasure, and each time they have been scared off as John Cooper rises from his grave to protect his booty.

## … AND MORE HIGHWAYMEN

*John Cooper was not the only highwayman in Buckinghamshire; in fact, the county was riddled with them. There were such fine houses throughout the county owned by so many well-to-do families who travelled frequently to London that the roads of Buckinghamshire made for rich pickings.*

On the way to Beaconsfield a party of travellers were going along, when a finely dressed and very handsome man with a romantic French accent asked to join them. Seeing how well presented the fellow was, the company thought he must be of noble blood and invited him to join their travelling party.

They chatted amiably for a while when the handsome stranger enquired if any of the party had been held up by a highwayman before.

'Thanks be to heaven, no sir,' they replied gratefully. The stranger said neither had he, but he had heard stories …

'I hear in Edlesborough many a poor victim has fallen to the greed of Jack Leather. He rides out every night to hunt for those travelling alone and takes their goods to the cry of 'Stand and Deliver', and with a pistol held to their heads. Can you just image it, madame: alone in the dark, dark night, the sounds of hooves rushing towards you, the blaze of the pistol in the night's gloom blinding you and then those rough hands searching your pockets, pulling your treasured jewels from your lily-white throat. How dreadful an ordeal. Oh, madame, I did not mean to fright you. Rest easy, for I hear the soldiers came to the farm where he works and, noticing that the horses were quite lathered first thing in the early morning, they caught him and strung him up at the gibbet on Ivinghoe Beacon.

'Ah, then there is that cad of a highwayman, stealing the glory of the other gentlemen of the road, that Dick Turpin. You don't want to believe what you hear about him, there is no decency to him at all. The fellow is a ruffian, trained as a butcher, and a butcher is what he has stayed – even murders his own men, they say.

I hear he rides through Edlesborough, too. There in Butler's Manor at Northall he watches from the attic window, spying upon wealthy travellers, which he then rides out to attack in the most violent and terrible of fashions. When they catch him and let him swing, I dare say he shall haunt those places where he committed such atrocities 'til the horns of heaven sound.

'Sir are you feeling well, you have gone quite pale?

'Then there is James Dormer, who became a highwayman in High Wycombe after winning a duel by boxing his opponent to death; he was then called a fugitive, and had to rob to survive.

'Ah, but do not think that we men are all bad, ladies, for you too can be the harbingers of highway horrors. The Wicked Lady is said on occasion to ride this way. The lady highwayman is reputed to be none other than the poor orphaned Lady Katherine Ferrers, who was married off young to a husband who had more of a mind to war than to her. Poor lady, never to have known the soft touch of a lover, that secure and safe harbour in a troubled world. No! For her only loss and hardship; her parents, her guardians, all gone and lost to that bloody civil war. And when she does marry, her husband takes her inheritance and sells it off piece by piece to pay for his silly games of being a soldier. I ask you, madame, what would you do as you see your money be stolen away from you? You'd steal it right back!

'So the lady came to dress herself in men's clothing and, whilst her husband was away so often playing boy soldier, Lady Ferrers took to the highways and byways. There she held the rich and noble, those who have squabbled over the right to rule and taken everything from her – her wealth, her family and her liberty – and she took it right back. What a woman! But then the lady got quite a taste for the power and soon robbery was not enough, and she took to burning down buildings, slaughtering the livestock of her enemies and even killed a constable who tried to arrest her.

'Alas, so much hardship in her life, so little love that the fair lady turned most terrible, soaked in the blood of her victims. Can you imagine? But, alas, the poor wench was shot one night when a hold-up went bad and, riding back to her safe haven, she arrived quite dead upon her horse. Her servants, seeing her in those highwayman's clothes, quickly took her in, washed her down and put her in more dignified attire before alerting the authorities to try to keep her secret safe. They say her ghost still haunts these roads, holding up unwary travellers such as ourselves … what was that? Did you hear something?

'Maybe nothing. Have you heard of John Shrimpton from Penn? No? Well, let me tell you, he is much more of an affable fellow; a likable rogue who has more brains and courage than most highwaymen. He was sent to London to apprentice as a soap-boiler but hated it. Whilst there, he fell in with a bad lot, took to pick-pocketing and stealing, and it wasn't long before he had a horse and returned to the well-known roads of his childhood to plunder coaches, horsemen and pedestrians. He once robbed an upstart of a barrister of fifty guineas at Stokenchurch and on another occasion he held up four stagecoaches all at once at Gerrards Cross and took a mighty £150; what a man to manage such a feat, eh! You may think him a villain, but still an impressive feat!

'But he was good too. One day he came upon two bailiffs dragging a poor farmer off to gaol for a debt of £6. John pulled the money from his own pocket and paid the debt, freeing the farmer, who was eternally grateful. A little further down the road those bailiffs were held up by the highwayman for the sum of £6. A Robin Hood, you might say!

'I hear one night he was in London, taking the night off and enjoying a bottle of wine, when a man sat at his table. They got to talking of this and that, when it turned out that the stranger was a hangman who had no idea he was talking to a highwayman; he droned on about how he would 'string 'em all up' if he could. John asked why the knot was placed upon the left side of the neck and not central, for surely this was a slower and ineffective way. The hangman suggested that if his drinking partner should ever need his services that he would be sure to place the knot centrally. John, beginning to feel the heat, said he would prefer not to require his services at all.

'But, alas, he was in Bristol one night and was rather the worse for wear after a night of drinking, and a constable tried to arrest him; in his bid to get away he murdered the night watchman, and despite several great men vouching for him, he was sent to the gibbet.

'And lastly, there is Claude Duval, you must have heard of him, eh? They say he is every bit the romantic image of a highwayman – as handsome as he is charming and daring. A Frenchman like myself, a good horseman, he came to England in the service of Charles II during the Restoration. Claude abhors violence and as far as possible never uses a weapon. They say he is a frequent visitor to the George Inn in Beaconsfield, where one night he had to fight his way out down the staircase, and swiftly got away. Where did you say you were staying when we reach Beaconsfield?'

'You know, young noble ladies were so taken with the stories of Claude that those in search for a bit of adventure would find reason to be travelling richly dressed and alone in the hopes of being accosted by the prince of highwaymen. It is said that one day, in broad daylight he held up a wealthy merchant and his pretty young wife. When he witnessed the dismissive way the merchant treated his wife, Claude said the merchant could keep some of his money in exchange for a dance with the lady. The merchant (being far more interested in his wealth) agreed, and so there on the road-side Claude danced with the wife. An intimate and longing dance! Afterwards, the highwayman was so disgusted by the merchant's treatment of his fair lady that he told the wealthy man to get his priorities right, for his wife was the true treasure and wealth of his life. All husbands should know that! Isn't that right, Sir? Does your wife like to dance?

'Ah, here we are, Beaconsfield, the George Inn.'

The travellers parted ways, terrified after the evening of highwaymen stories they had endured. Most of the travellers headed into the George for accommodation for the night, but one man – a farmer, whose purse was heavy with coin from his day's trading – headed off home to his farm on the edge of Beaconsfield. As he walked the dark route alone, those tales of robbery and dastardly figures in the night played on his mind. So, when a figure suddenly appeared before him dressed elegantly in black and demanding his money, he was so frightened he handed over his purse without question. The highwayman took the purse, opened it, and taking 100 sovereigns, threw the rest back to the farmer and disappeared into the gloom of the night. It was only afterwards when the farmer thought on the experience that he realised there had been no weapons and that the French accent of the highwayman had sounded rather familiar.

## The Water's Warning

*Water is usually thought of as pure and because of this it has often been used in divination going back through the ages. In this case, it is a local belief that the course and surge of the waters of the Misbourne River have the power of foresight.*

A gypsy woman was making her way home to Great Missenden by riding through the beech wood, when she saw her friend Mrs Lee hurrying in the opposite direction, looking quite affrighted and anxious. The gypsy woman halted her pony cart and asked if her friend was all right.

Mrs Lee looked at her friend with worried eyes and told her that their folk were all on the move. Trouble was coming; she had seen it in the waters of the Misbourne, which were full and angry. 'It will come from the east, that's what Misbourne is saying. Misbourne always knows when the black luck is on the land.'

This was a grave warning indeed, for those with a local memory knew that the Misbourne had foretold many a great sorrow to befall all England, for the waters had risen and flooded just before the great sickness of the Plague in 1665, and for the Fire of London the following year. They had

risen for King Edward VII's death, and for the start of the Great War. The people knew that if the Misbourne rose then trouble was soon to follow.

Mrs Lee, eager not to tarry any longer, bade her friend farewell and slipped away westward through the trees, placing as much distance between herself and the river as she could before nightfall. The gypsy, mindful of the warning but now more impatient than ever to get home, hurried on her way. By the time she arrived, the ponies were tired for she had pushed them hard after the warning. She quickly stabled them and got herself inside.

Moments later, an eerie droning sounded out across the land, a harrowing hum that struck a fear into all those who heard it. The first sirens were wailing to signal the start of the Blitz.

# DRAGON'S POND

*Dragons have always fascinated the imagination, whether in regional folk tales or universal myths and legends. Sometimes they represent evil and at other times wisdom or luck. During the Middle Ages, dragons came to be a creature associated with paganism and devil worship, so it was every good Christian's duty to slay the beast. Yet many of these tales also show dragons to be soothed or even tamed by the women. Most European dragons are associated with the elements of fire and earth, and here we have an unusual case of a water dragon.*

Half a mile or so from the church at Hughenden, there stands a house that was once used as a Knights Templar Hospital. In that house there was a young servant woman whose daily job it was to go out to the pond to fetch water. To reach the pond she had to carry her buckets past a copse of trees, bushes, and briars, which surrounded the pond and kept it secluded.

Now work in the house was hard and the days were long. The young woman had to get up early each morning, sometimes even before the sun had risen, to begin cleaning out the fires, tidying the house, and collecting the water for washing, cleaning, and cooking. That is why she always found herself lingering on her walk to the pond, where she would sit down by the water's edge for a few moments of peace and quiet by herself to rest and enjoy the day. Due to the seclusion of the pond by the briars, she felt quite safe that nobody would see her as she tarried.

The day it happened was not a particularly remarkable day. She had got up just like any other day, dressed herself, and began her chores. Of course, the cook shouted and yelled, but that was normal, so she had picked up her buckets and gone out to fetch water. As she made her way past the trees, she noticed the day was unusually quiet, even the birds that so often filled the air with their song seemed to be gone. She thought, 'perhaps a hawk is around today, so the birds are away hiding'. Humming to herself, she came to the edge of the cool pond. Putting her buckets down, she knelt beside the water's edge, running her fingers across the glittering surface. So lost in her own thoughts was she, that she didn't notice the movement in the briars on the far edge of the pond. Something had slithered out of the bushes, slipped into the water and even now was making its way towards her underneath the surface.

The water around the woman's fingers started to ripple so she peered down into the water and saw a pair of eyes staring back. The woman looked again but the eyes had gone. The woman stopped humming and she moved away from the water's edge and sat quietly. A few moments later, a great water serpent's scaly head rose from the depths of the pond and looked straight at the girl. In fright, she leapt up and ran back through the trees but, just as she was nearing the house, she realised that she had left the buckets by the pond. For that alone she would be in for a good hiding from the cook and no supper.

For a moment she stood there wondering what to do as the creature had been of such an immense size, though it had not advanced on her.

But the young woman, who had grown up with hardships and had seen difficult times, was stout of heart. Therefore, she grabbed a handful of scraps from the kitchen without being seen and shoved them in her apron pocket and cautiously made her way back to the pond. She peered through the briars, and saw the dragon nudging at the buckets, pushing them into the water and beginning to play with them around the surface of the pond. Carefully she stepped out of the bushes, and the dragon turned to look at her. She pulled the scraps from her pocket and threw them to the other side of the pond. The dragon paused for a moment, uncertain what to do, but then tasting the air with its tongue it sensed the food and turned towards it. Quick as a flash, the girl ran forward grabbed her buckets and made her way back to the house.

The rest of the day passed in a whirl as her earlier adventure played itself over and over in her mind. The next day she was up bright and early, and no matter how much the cook shouted it didn't dampen her mood. When she grabbed the buckets that morning, she made sure to steal a few slices of meat and a sweet cake, which she popped into her pocket and made her way to the pond. When she arrived, the water seemed still; nothing seemed to be around, though the birds were still not singing. Before going near the water's edge, the girl took out the scraps and threw them into the pond. Suddenly the water bubbled and churned as the dragon snapped up the scraps, its great serpent's eye watching her carefully. She approached the pond carefully, both young woman and water serpent warily watching each other. Without taking her eyes off the beast, she slowly lowered the buckets down into the water to fill them. The dragon's scales quivered slightly as its muscles rippled but it stayed where it was watching.

And that was the way of it. Each day, she would take scraps and each day they would carefully watch each other, neither approaching the other but neither quite trusting the other. Some days she would go to the pond and the birds would be singing and she would know that her scaly associate would not be around that day, and other times the lack of birdsong warned her to be careful. She saw the dragon so frequently that she almost forgot how unusual the situation was. In time, she took to sitting a safe distance off near the briars and hummed whilst her cautious dragon watched her, its head curled out of the water as if to listen better.

Spring gave way to summer, when even more water was needed. Soon after, the leaves on the trees began to create a warm palette of reds, oranges and yellows, until the leaves fell to create an autumn blanket upon the ground. It seemed to the girl that winter came early that year. The snows fell suddenly, and the surface of the pond began to freeze. As the weather got colder, she saw less of her unusual poolside companion and she hoped that it had found somewhere warm to weather out the winter.

It was one of the first days of spring, when the sky was a clear blue and the sun cast down a golden light upon the grass, which seemed to renew its greenness. The ice on the pond had melted weeks ago and, though there was still an icy bite to the air, it felt as though the seasons were turning once again. The girl had not seen her dragon for a while, the bitter snows having kept it away, so on this day she had not noticed the silence in the air. She sat down by the water's edge, lost in her thoughts, trailing her fingers through the water, when she saw an enormous shape beneath. The dragon was back, she thought to herself, and she was strangely happy to see it. But something in its glare frightened her, and she flung herself back just in time to see its great jaw snapping at the very place that she had been. The young woman scuttled backwards away from the beast, whose long scaly body rose from the water, its gaping jaws revealing its long teeth and forked tongue. She scrambled to her feet and pushed her way through the briars, though the thorns tore at her skirt and skin. This time, not stopping to care about the buckets, she ran straight back to the house.

The cook began to rage that there were no buckets of water, but then seeing the young woman's face, stopped and asked what the matter was. The young woman told her story of the water serpent who she'd seen frequently, and though it had never been a threat before, such a beast of uncommon size advancing upon her had frightened her so that she dared not go back to the pond for fear of her very life. Word soon spread and others came to question the girl, and so she told her story again and again. People wanted to know why she hadn't told them sooner that such a dangerous beast was living in their midst. She tried to insist that it hadn't been dangerous beforehand and that she couldn't understand why the beast had turned so ferocious towards her now. Amongst those that were gathered was a cleric who was wise in the ways of beasts and muttered in Latin, 'quarum vis inopia cibi acrier'.

'Pardon?' said the young woman.

'Oh, the beast turned on you because of the strength of its hunger due to the scarcity of food over the winter; just waking up, it needs to feed.'

'That might be as so,' called out a stout man, a forester. 'But if it has the thinking you look like dinner, then who is next? It's got to go.'

'Besides,' mumbled the cook, 'if there be a water serpent it will bring bad luck upon all of us.'

So, the neighbours gathered together to create a plan. The beast must surely be lured into the open where it could be dealt with. It seemed to respond to the young woman, and so they told her to go and sit next to the pond while they waited in the bushes. The young woman wanted no part of it, but she didn't want anyone to get hurt either, so with the men armed with bows and spears, they walked passed the trees and she edged her way towards the water's edge. In her heart she hoped the dragon would not be there that day. In her head she tried to call out, 'Hide!'

As the water began to ripple, she knew it was too late, and the water serpent rose from the surface, turning to look at the young woman. Neither moved as they just watched one another, until a terrible humming cut through the air. A spear pierced the dragon's neck, and it began to flail in the water, letting out a terrible sound as it did so. Then another spear found its mark. The woman could not bear to watch as the beast faltered, and she ran back to the house, tears flowing down her cheeks.

She hid herself away, but a short time later there came the sound of great carousing as the men made their way back to the house carrying their fallen foe upon their shoulders. They sang themselves great songs of victory and told the story of how bravely they had fought and defeated the beast, while they feasted that night. But the young woman had no appetite. The next morning those heroes skinned the dragon and stuffed its hide with straw to hang it outside the house to show all who came there how terrible the beast had been. It remained there for a long time until the skin was finally claimed by the wind, and the rain, and the sun. Then, so that it would not be forgotten, the story was painted on the wall of the hall so everyone would remember the Dragon in the Pond.

There was only one person who wished she could forget.

## THE GREEN MAN OF FINGEST

*In years gone by, the county of Buckinghamshire fell under the diocese of Lincoln, which meant that much of the Buckinghamshire countryside and estates were owned by the*

*Church and often used as the residential homes for important bishops. This is how in 1330 the Bishop of Lincoln, Henry de Burghest (sometimes written as Burgwash), came to be in possession of Fingest Manor. In those days the local estate and manor owned much of the land surrounding it, which was known as its park. This land was often rented out to the folk who lived within the estate's boundaries for the grazing of their herds of cows, sheep, and pigs or for farming. This is how life had been for generations in Fingest; the people looking after the land, and the Lord of the Manor tended to the people.*

Bishop Henry de Burghest had a reputation that preceded him. He had risen through the ranks of the ecclesiastical orders not by piety but through sheer ambition. He was a man for whom the Church had been a route to power, money, and a very comfortable lifestyle. It was said of him that he was a 'covetous, rebellious, ambitious and injurious' man who was 'neither good for church, nor state, sovereign, nor subjects'. During his life he was the chancellor once, lord treasurer twice, and was once sent as an ambassador to Bavaria – one wonders what his diplomatic charm may have been like as he was described so differently. It is fair to say Bishop Henry de Burghest was not a loved or even liked man, but one not to be dallied with, for he used his power to his own ends.

Fingest Manor stood near the church, as did so many Norman manors. It was a small, plain building, not like the impressive palace at Woburn, which was also owned by the diocese of Lincoln. So, it surprised many, but was a blessed relief, when Bishop Henry decided to live in Fingest Manor, far away from polite society. So why did he choose a small, plain manor? For a man who loved to show off his might and wealth it may indeed seem odd, but Fingest was near good hunting grounds, and Bishop Henry loved nothing more than to head the hunt.

It was not long before the common folk of Fingest found their new neighbour was causing upset, from generally unpleasant behaviour to outright hostility, but matters were only going to get worse. Bishop Henry disliked all these common folks using his land for their dirty animals, and their peasant crops. He wanted to keep out the villains (an old term for villagers) and use the parkland to hunt. So, he enclosed the park, seizing 300 acres of it for himself, leaving only 100 acres for the sixty families of Fingest to survive on and depriving them of the common land they had used for years, and their families had used before them.

The people were furious; they attempted to have it out with him, but he would not hold a council with them, so finally the common folk made complaints against Bishop Henry to the Church, but the bishop was a powerful man and so the case was always found in his favour. His disagreeable personality and his greed caused strife between him and the local people at Fingest right up until his death in 1340.

Although they didn't get their land back, at least the terrible bishop was gone, and surely things could get no worse. But shortly after Bishop Henry was buried, rumour started to abound throughout the local area that his ghost had been seen wandering around the parkland, Hanger Wood to Mill Hanging Lane, and from the manor to the church. It seems that even death could not stop the abysmal bishop, and people were afraid thinking that he'd come back to cause even more mischief in his ghostly form. They avoided the areas where his ghost had been spotted: the woodlands and hunting forest, and around the parkland of his estate.

For all the woe and fear Bishop Henry had caused, there were still some amongst the local folk who were prepared to take on the ghostly apparition. Sharing a few beers, some of the younger fellows egged each other on. One man complained: 'Alive, that blasted bishop made our lives a misery and, now he is dead, half the village are afeared of going out after dark.'

Another replied, 'It ain't right, we should do something.'

'Yes!' cried the youngest amongst them. 'If he had a body to hit, I'd walk up to him and teach him a lesson to take to the other side of the grave.'

The others nodded and congratulated the lad on his good idea. That was exactly what someone should do, and wasn't he just the man to do it. With a few more beers inside, the lad felt as fierce as a bear, and with his friends to back him up that is what he would do. Yet, a little way outside the tavern, one friend remembered he had to be up early and hurried home; another said he had to check his sheep; and another two said they would watch from the bushes … a safe distance away. So, by the time they reached the road on the edge of the woodlands by Fingest Manor, the young lad stood alone in the moonlight.

As the cold night air seeped into his bones, the beer bravado ebbed away; the lad's knees started to knock and, despite the chill, he began to sweat. It was then that the air suddenly got colder, and the lad saw his own breath. Everything went silent and time seemed to stop. Out of the woods a green shimmering mist seemed to form, and as it approached the lad the form became more solid and a moaning filled the air. Walking, or perhaps better to describe as floating, the bishop's ghost appeared dressed all in green, holding out his hands to the lad. The ghost moaned and started to form words: 'Help me … tell Lincoln to free the land.'

That was more than enough for anyone to take and the lad ran for his life. When he and his friends recovered in the morning, they told their tale: 'It was definitely the bishop', 'he was all sorrowful looking', 'he was holding out his hands like he was begging of me – he wants the land to be returned to us', 'Well, looks like the ole sinner got his comeuppance.'

These recounts and others soon spread, all saying the bishop was begging the local people to go to Lincoln and get the enclosed land returned to common use. A former colleague of the bishop was sent to investigate the stories and met with Bishop Henry's squire, who had seen his recently departed master most evenings. The churchman heard the tales and asked the squire to take him to the place where the ghostly bishop wandered, which the squire nervously agreed to do, and there they waited to see if their old associate would appear. Being a man of faith, the investigator waited patiently until the green mist appeared, gathering form as it approached until there in front of the waiting men stood the bishop, all in green forester attire with a bow, quiver, and horn slung around his person.

'Be you a devil sent from hell in the guise of a holy man?' questioned the investigator.

'I was once the Bishop of Lincoln, Henry Burghest, and as such I committed evil against my fellow man. I had little care for the people or the world around me. I enclosed these lands and made the folk, animals, and land all suffer for my greed. As my penance I am compelled to wander as the spirit of this place, the park keeper until all is set right. Friend, go to Lincoln; tell them it's God's will these lands are rightfully returned, and in doing so you may save my soul also.'

As his words faded in the air, so did the visage of the spectre until the investigator stood alone.

This was reported back to the ecclesiastical court in Lincoln, and it was ruled that William Bachelor would undertake the process of returning the property back to common use. So, it was that the enclosures came down, the people got their land back, and the ghost of Bishop Henry became forever quiet.

*The cynic might suspect that these stories were started by the locals in order to get their land back, but so many people spoke of seeing Bishop Henry in his ghostly form, and the story spread so far and wide, that it seemed to prove the tale to be true. There has also been a 'Black Dog' ghostly hound seen lurking on Fingest Lane over the years, which are sometimes connected to Green Man or Wild Hunt stories. Sightings of the Green Man of Fingest have been recounted in the area, and right up to Hughenden Valley, throughout the ages – the most recent accounts in 1986. Is this still the bishop paying his penance or is some other soul compelled to become the spirit of the forest to atone for past sins?*

## THE CHURCH MYSTERY

*Throughout the county there are a number of 'moving church' stories; some reveal the mystery mover, others leave it up to your imagination. The origins of St Lawrence are suitably shrouded in mystery considering its later connections to the Hellfire Club.*

The plans had been made and the officials had set the date: West Wycombe was to get a new church, dedicated to St Lawrence. It was to be built at the foot of the hill, and so the materials were gathered, the foundation stone was laid, and building began.

At the end of the first day the builders were pleased with their progress and off they went to rest their weary bones. The sun rose bright the next morning, it would be a good day for building, and the workers returned to the site, but when they came to the foot of the hill there were no foundations or materials to be seen. The space where the church was supposed to be was empty.

Looking around with some confusion, the builders discovered that their work had been moved to the very top of the hill. This was most strange, who would have done such a thing? A lot of questions were asked, but no one had seen or heard anything, and the movement must have happened in the dead of night, so all agreed it must be some supernatural force. The only question then was … was it fairies, devils or angels who had moved the church?

The builders decided to move the materials for the church back down the hill and set to work re-laying the foundations, but at the end of a long day they were further behind than they had been the day before. Tired and frustrated, they went to their beds.

When they came to their workings the next day, sure enough, the foundations had been moved back up to the top of the hill. Well, after a few days of this carrying on it was just too strange, and the workmen refused to continue until a priest had been fetched.

The priest came with a candle, a bell and a Bible. Chanting, he exorcised the workings both at the top of the hill and the foot of the hill until he assured everybody that whatever demons might be at play, they were now banished.

It was then that an unearthly voice echoed across the hill, promising never to annoy or harm the people of West Wycombe ever again if the church was built on the top of the hill.

With even the priest unable to stop strange events occurring, the people of West Wycombe decided it was best to do as the voice said; and so it was that West Wycombe church was built on the top of the hill, where it stands to this very day.

*Years after its construction, the local nobleman Sir Francis Dashwood, founder of the Hellfire Club, designed and had constructed a golden globe to sit atop St Lawrence. The globe is hollow and large enough to fit nine people inside. It was here that the Hellfire Club met to share card nights, but sometimes these evenings turn into outrageous parties, and when the members brought along their lovers, orgies rocked that golden globe. That orb must have created many a memorable evening for the members because, even after their deaths, the sound of raucous parties and ghostly figures playing cards have been encountered.*

When the golden globe was first put in place, there was a flagstaff proudly protruding from the top of it. One day in 1743, a sailor who was home from duty was missing the adventure of the ocean waves. He had been telling a few of his boyhood friends about his duties on board the ship, and he got to telling them about climbing the rigging, and how he was the best climber on ship; that he could climb a flagpole straight up if he chose. They laughed and with their tongues in cheeks nodded and exclaimed, 'Ah, right.' Being somewhat affronted by his friends' disbelief, the sailor took it upon himself to show these landlubbers how good he was.

Away to the church they went, and to a gathering crowd the sailor proved his skill as he climbed the globe, then the flagpole, resting his chin upon the top of it. The watching crowd gave a mighty cheer, and the sailor returned to the ground to a hero's welcome. For weeks afterwards, he continued to boast that not one among his former friends and neighbours could achieve such a feat, as Neptune only blessed those who travel his seas with such prowess.

Well, one William Rolfe was not going to let that lie.

'We here country boys are every bit as skilled as ye. Aye, working on those vast ships out at sea for months on end be hard graft, but working the fields, or yielding the hammer at the smithy be tough in their own ways, too. Landlubbers we may be, but weak and foolish we aint!'

And to prove his words, William climbed the globe, and then the pole and, to a mighty cheer – much louder than the first – William placed his chin on the top of the pole. If the locals of West Wycombe had celebrated their seafaring son, then they revelled and rejoiced when their son born and bred achieved the same. So, it was thusly settled that Neptune gave no more special abilities than the gods of field and forge did.

## MAD MONKS OF MEDMENHAM

*Much has been speculated on the activities that occurred as part of the Hellfire Club, and there are plenty of books on the subject. Some say the stories are exaggerations; others say the rumours play down the strange and unnatural events that did indeed take place. Whatever the truth, the Hellfire Club has certainly passed into folklore.*

When Sir Francis Dashwood was only sixteen, his father died, leaving him a vast fortune and West Wycombe Park. In the years following, Sir Francis proved to be a well-liked man full of mirth and enjoyment, showing impeccable loyalty to his friends. As a wealthy local landowner, he believed he had a responsibility to those less well-off than himself, and as Chancellor of the Exchequer he sought ways to lessen the unemployment situation. But these accreditations are not the reasons why the Second Baronet Sir Francis Dashwood has gone down in history.

For many young noblemen of the era, it was quite fashionable to take Grand Tours around Europe or even further afield. Usually these trips would be taken with close friends to explore the bounty of art, architecture, culture and cuisine of other places, particularly those of antiquity like Rome and Greece. Sir Francis found his own Grand Tour life-changing. His time in Italy diminished his Christian beliefs, and at the same time his fascination with antiquarian mythology grew through the heritage of stories, paintings, sculptures and culture. This, along with the friendships he made on that trip, were to set him on a path that would forever make him infamous.

On the Grand Tour the friends enjoyed fine food, sumptuous wine and the many treasures of paintings and sculptures. So, upon his return in 1733, Sir Francis set up a dining club for fine gentlemen interested in Italian art called the Dilettanti Society, and the dress code was togas. In 1744 he set up yet another group called the Divan Club, for those who had visited the Ottoman Empire, and here everyone who attended was robed in 'Turkish garb'.

But the club he is most famous for forming is the Hellfire Club, which was created to celebrate liberty and friendship, or as John Wilkes MP (one of the Hellfire Club members) puts it: 'a set of worthy, jolly fellows, happy disciples of Venus and Bacchus, [who] got occasionally together to celebrate woman in wine and to give more zest to the festive meeting, they plucked every luxurious idea from the ancients and enriched their own modern pleasures with the tradition of classic luxury.'

It started in the George and Vulture in London and was never called the Hellfire Club by its members – this was so named by those who were scandalised by the stories that arose from the mystery surrounding the activities of the club. So, Sir Francis began looking for a more secluded home for his new club and became interested in Medmenham Abbey, which was six miles from West Wycombe Park.

The monks had left years ago and now the abbey was in a ruinous state, but the leaseholders (the Duffields) had built an Elizabethan house on the site. Sir Francis Dashwood then set about restoring the manor house and returning the monks to Medmenham. However, the brotherhood he had in mind was no holy order but the 'Knights of St Francis of Wycombe' … the Hellfire Club.

The club was exclusive and only ever had thirteen members at any one time, although the list of members included the most powerful, even the nobility. During meetings of the club, lavish feasts with many toasts would be shared by its members, all of whom were permitted to bring a lovely lady – as long as she had a jolly temperament. These women were far from strumpets but considered themselves the true wives of the Mad Monks of Medmenham. The members of the order were bound by strict rules that no brother would interfere or act indecently towards another brother's lady. In its later years, the club moved from Medmenham to the now famous caves that were excavated out of the open chalk quarry in West Wycombe. The chalk had been removed, not just for the purpose of creating deep tunnels, a banqueting hall, a mock 'River Styx' and an inner temple that lay directly under St Lawrence Church, but to improve the local roads and provide employment for locals who had suffered three failed harvests. In fact, it was said Sir Francis hired many more men than he needed and, rather than choosing to open quarry the chalk, he choose to tunnel, which was a much longer process. He paid these men one shilling a day – quite a wage in those days – which provided a lifeline for many local families as the harvest had repeatedly failed in recent years. Sir Francis and his club had a notorious reputation for being devil worshippers (although why a devil worshipper would have spent so much money on restoring the church does make one wonder) and of the most corrupt and debauched nature. In truth, what went on in those meetings we shall never know, but they do provide for some wonderful stories.

The meetings of the Hellfire Club (from what details can be gathered) seem to have been elaborate affairs with each of the members dressed in full costume of white monks' robes, and the 'Prior' wearing a red bonnet. A great feast would be had with many toasts and with lots of wine (and other such beverages) being consumed in large amounts. When the feast was finally over then the members would return to their 'cells'. What followed was often a mockery of Roman Catholic ceremonies, involving the idea of mirth, whether that was in the form of practical jokes on fellow members, getting drunk or enjoying the 'company' of their ladies.

At one of the annual gatherings, John Wilkes had decided to play a practical joke on the Earl of Sandwich that involved a considerable amount of planning.

Throughout the meal, Wilkes made sure he had not over-indulged in drinking, so that when he returned to his cell he dressed quickly for the ceremony, and then he collected a great baboon he had hidden the night before. Wilkes dressed the baboon in clothes to make it look like the devil and then stealthily hurried along to the temple.

Once there, he opened the chest that had contained all the ceremonial objects (now already placed in anticipation of the upcoming proceedings) and put the baboon inside, closing the lid and securing it with a cord. Wilkes then carefully laid this cord under the carpet up to his own chair that he used in the ceremonies and, having had a secret hole drilled in it for the cord so he could tug upon it without being seen, his trap was laid.

He hurried back to his cell and awaited the call to ceremony, which came soon after. All the brethren filed into the space and the ceremony began. Leading the service was the Earl of Sandwich, and at the desired moment Wilkes pulled on the cord.

All at once the lid of the chest sprang open, the baboon burst forth and leapt upon the back of Lord Sandwich, who in shock turned to see the grinning (apes grin when scared) devil-dressed creature on his back. Terror pulsed through him as he tried to shake the demon from his back, but the more he tried to free himself, the more the alarmed ape clung on. It seemed to Lord Sandwich that all the tomfoolery calling upon the devil had worked. Here he was, come now to collect their souls. The poor fear-wracked man cried out:

'Spare me, gracious devil! Spare a wretch who never was sincerely your servant. I sinned only from vanity of being in the fashion; thou knowest I never have been half so wicked as I pretended: never have been able to commit the thousandth part of the vices which I have boasted of … leave me, therefore, and go to those who are more truly devoted to your service. I am but half a sinner …'

With that, Lord Sandwich ran out screaming, much to the hilarity of other members. From that day forth, Wilkes and Lord Sandwich had an ongoing vendetta.

*The Hellfire Club ran for twenty years and is now a subject of rumours, mystery and intrigue. The stories of scandal surrounding it are not the only thing to haunt the caves of the Hellfire Club. The grounds around the area are said to be haunted by a glowing ghostly-blue woman and a maid; perhaps these are some of the women who took part in the strange activities in the caves, or maybe they relate to the next story.*

## SUKIE'S LOVE

*Near the Hellfire Club caves in West Wycombe there was an inn called the George and Dragon. It still operates to this day, though now it is the George and Dragon Hotel with fine rooms to take a short break in, or stop for lunch, while visiting the nearby Hellfire Caves.*

Many years ago, there was a young friendly lass whose name was Sukie and she worked at the George and Dragon inn as a barmaid and serving wench. She may have been only sixteen years old, but Sukie was a beautiful, buxom blonde bombshell and knew how to attract the men. Sukie knew exactly what she wanted out of life. She was not going to marry a farm hand or one of the local lads, oh no! She had her eye on marrying a man from a higher social standing, and the tavern was a perfect place to meet such men.

Sukie liked to work barefoot and hated the modest dull dresses she was forced to wear by the wife of the landlord. She shared the attic space with two other serving girls but often after she had finished work, she would meet up with some lover or another down in the stables. Sukie tested her romantic skills upon the local lads, flirting, teasing them, even meeting up with them for passionate nights, but her eye was always for the refined gentleman.

One night, such a nobleman entered the George and Dragon. He was tall and handsome, every inch of him cut the fine figure of a 'gentle' man, and Sukie noticed him immediately. The other girls also took notice – it was hard not to – and immediately they gossiped that he must be one of those gentlemen who partook in Sir Francis Dashwood's notorious Hellfire Club. Sukie had heard the rumours of those fine gentlemen and their mistresses, and couldn't imagine anything more exciting. Sukie told the other girls that she would serve his table tonight, and any other night he came in, and if they so much as even thought about waiting on him there would be a reckoning to be had!

She walked over, putting on a well-rehearsed performance, appearing to have every bit the gentle graces of a lady. She gave the nobleman her sweetest smile and took his order for a meal and ale, which she oversaw herself to make sure everything was just right. Soon she was back at his side with his food, and Sukie kept the man company while he ate. In no time at all, the nobleman was smitten and when she was called to do other chores, his eyes never left her, no matter where she was in the room.

When the nobleman left that night, Sukie felt she was dancing on air. But not everyone was so happy. Three local lads, all of whom had been a lover of Sukie's at one time or another, had seen the whole charade. Normally she would come and chat to them or flirt with them, maybe even end up in the hay barn with one of them, but that night all she done was dote on that rich fool.

The next night, Sukie went about her work. The three spurned lovers were in an aggrieved mood and did nothing but hassle her and annoy her all night. So when, just before closing, the nobleman arrived, Sukie's heart skipped a beat. When her work has done, she met up with the nobleman and they spoke, just spoke, which made Sukie fall ever more in love with him.

Over the next few weeks, the nobleman would come as often as he could. For a few nights he would be there every evening, and then a day or two would pass and she would see nothing of him. These were the days that felt so grey. Throughout this time, the three spurned lovers became more and more jealous and they started to hatch a plan to teach that Sukie a lesson.

In all the time she had spent with her lover, Sukie was convinced of his nobility, and that he must surely be one of the members of the strange Hellfire Club which she'd heard so many exciting rumours about. She started to imagine being taken along to these strange ceremonies; how she would love that, how she would be adored, and what fine dresses she would wear.

When the stable lad arrived with a letter one day saying
it was from her nobleman whom she had not seen for a few
nights, Sukie grabbed it immediately and ran off to open it.
She read the letter with hungry eyes, and then reread it, once,
twice, thrice. With delight, she read that he asked her to come
away with him and for her to meet him at the caves in a dress
of white on the following night. It seemed to confirm all of
her hopes, and now her dreams were coming true.

She could think of nothing else all day. She went about
her work almost forgetting what it was that she was doing.
Those three local lads where just as awful and annoying as
ever; what had she seen in them? But now she was going
to show them. She was going to marry her nobleman and
become a fine lady.

That night, as soon as the tavern was closed, she slipped
out to the stables where she had hidden her dress, changed
quickly and, making sure that nobody was following her,
Sukie made her way to the caves of the Hellfire Club. It was
dark, it was difficult to see, and there seemed to be no lamp-
light ahead as might be expected from a waiting lover, and so
she began to call out to her nobleman.

Just as she approached the mouth of the cave, surrounded
by the great imposing Gothic follies, there was the sound of
footsteps behind her. She turned expecting to see her handsome man but there instead were her three spurned lovers.
They laughed at her horribly, called her stupid for imagining
that a nobleman would want to marry her, and then they
threw themselves at her clawing at her hair, tearing her dress.
She was terrified by the attack, tears tumbling down her face.
She tried to fight them off and managed to pull away from
their grasp. As she ran away, she fell and cracked her head
upon a rock, which killed her instantly.

The three lads, realising what they done, quickly picked
up her body and ran back to the George and Dragon,

raising the alarm but fleeing before they could get caught. So Sukie was found in a terrible state; the doctor was called for, but there was nothing that could be done, so the poor girl was buried.

Yet, a week later Sukie was seen back serving at the bar, her beautiful blonde head flirtatiously bobbing between customers, invisibly moving pots and pans, and pints around the inn. And so Sukie has been seen haunting the George and Dragon ever since. Maybe she's waiting for her nobleman to return?

## THE AMERSHAM MARTYRS

*The London Road (A355) runs through the old part of Amersham, a pretty place to wander. Amersham was once a small rural town along this one road, which cut through the Market Place, and is now where the Amersham Museum can be found. Going up the hill out of the old town on the London Road, the Chequers Inn can still be found to quench the thirst and fill the stomachs of weary travellers and local alike. However, if you visit, keep your ears open for you may hear strange things that belie the dark past of this now pretty town.*

In the 1300s there was an Oxford scholar whose name was John Wycliffe. He believed that the Church had lost its way, becoming overly concerned with power, wealth and hierarchy, and that confession, pilgrimage and the worship of saints all distracted from the true worship of God. At this time, Bibles and church sermons were all in Latin, which was a language only accessible to the wealthy, powerful, and noble. John Wycliffe firmly believed that the Bible should be accessible to everybody, and that it should be written in English so that every man no matter his station could read and listen to the lessons held within. He created a translation of the Bible into English, and this made him incredibly unpopular with the powerful bishops.

When Henry VI came to the throne, he gave the Church, and especially the bishops, more power to convict heretics (people who did not follow the true Catholic faith as outlined by the King himself and his bishops). With this rule heretics could even be burnt at the stake.

Therefore, it was not John Wycliffe who felt the true force of the bishops' wrath as he had died peacefully as an old man years before. It was his followers who were to suffer the worst. Many supported Wycliffe's beliefs, especially about the importance of an English Bible. These followers called themselves the 'Justfast Men' or 'Known Men' because of their firm and steady allegiance to a clear and honest worship of God. Others, however, used a more contemptuous term, they called them the Lollards.

In the small market town of Amersham, out of the 900-strong population, were many Lollards in possession of English Bibles. Despite their differences in faith, the people of Amersham got along and mostly times were peaceful. Thomas Chase was the leader of the Amersham Lollards, and he and his flock would meet to read the Bible in English and concern themselves with how best to serve God in their everyday life. Thomas knew his fellow 'Known Men' well, amongst them was William Tylsworth and his family, including his daughter Joan Clerke, who had grown up reading the Bible.

This peaceful life of community acceptance, however, was about to change. In 1506, Bishop William Smith was given the job of searching out heretics. When Bishop Smith's investigators arrived in 1511, they caused fear and suspicion as they scourged the town, capturing Thomas Chase and charging sixty residents with heresy, including William and Joan. Those arrested were subjected to brutal treatment, forcing most of them to recount their beliefs and to suffer humiliating public punishment to prove that they had changed their faith. Some were forced to go on pilgrimage to Lincoln or Ashridge Abbey, where there was believed to be a phial of Christ's blood. Others were forced to wear heretic badges on their clothes, some had to carry a bundle of sticks up on their back every market day, and some were quite literally 'branded a heretic' with a red-hot iron upon their cheeks to mark them for life.

Thomas Chase was put through terrible torture to try and make him recant, for Bishop Smith knew if he could break Thomas, and get him to abandon his faith, then – as leader of the local Lollards – the others would lose faith soon after. Poor Thomas was taken to the bishop's palace at Woburn, and there put into the bishop's own prison, 'Little Ease'. It was Little Ease by name and nature, for he suffered constant beatings, strangling and starvation. Thomas was forced to attend the trials and punishments with a faggot of sticks tied to his back to show everyone that he would be for the pyre if he didn't repent. He endured three years of suffering in that prison, but not once did he renounce his faith. He stayed true to his beliefs, and still imprisoned he died in 1514. Some say he was strangled, others that he took his own life, but either way the cruelty inflicted upon him was the cause of his death.

William Tylsworth also did not repent, but there was no value in his renouncement, and so Bishop Smith decided to make an example of him. William was taken from the dark, cold prison and held overnight in the Chequers Inn, which by comparison must have been a welcome respite. However, William knew that his night at the inn would be his last on this earth and he was left to contemplate the terrible ordeal that was about to befall him. The following morning, he was taken to a hill (Rectory Hill), high above the town so everyone could see what happened to Lollards. There waiting for him was a stack of wood, with a stake standing tall in the centre.

Fear gripped William's heart and his limbs moved slowly as he was pushed forward. He was tied to a stake with a rough rope that bit into his flesh. As the crowd watched in horrified silence, William saw his own daughter Joan dragged forward; if it was not enough that he was going to suffer such a terrible fate it appeared as if his daughter would have to share it too. But no, Bishop Smith had something far worse in mind, for on that terrible morning William watched on as his daughter was tormented and forced to light the pyre of her own father's execution herself. As the flames began to reach upwards, William's clothes caught fire and his last sight as he screamed through the pain was to see Joan being forced to watch his agonising death by her own hand. In the years that followed Joan went mad with grief and guilt.

After such horrors, the town of Amersham was left in peace, and after a time the dreadfulness of those events began to settle. That is, until 1521, when Bishop John Longland, (Henry VIII's Royal Confessor) investigated the case of the Amersham Lollards and wondered if, ten years on, they had truly learnt their lesson. He dispatched his investigators back to Amersham. Upon seeing the investigators return, the terrible memories of what happened before returned. This was enough to send some fleeing and trying to escape, although they were often caught. One man, Thomas Holmes, was so terrified of what would happen that he tried to bargain his own life for the lives of others and denounced sixty of his fellow Lollards to the investigators. By the time the investigation was complete, one quarter of the population had been incriminated as Lollards. Many, like those ten years earlier, abandoned their faith and suffered the humiliating punishments.

However, Bishop Longland wanted to stamp out the Lollards once and for all, so he condemned six people to burn at the stake at Ruccles Field: one woman, Joan Norman, and five men – John Scrivener, James Morden, Robert Rave, Thomas Barnard, and Thomas Holmes, whom it would seem failed in saving his own life by betraying the rest of his town. The first, John Scrivener (like William Tylsworth), was forced to see his own children bullied and forced into lighting his pyre before he died in the torment of the flames. Throughout all this, Bishop Longland preached a sermon on the gravity of heresy.

The last Amersham Lollard heretic to be burnt was Thomas Harding, who had been previously convicted in both 1511 and 1521; he was burnt at Chesham in 1532 for owning an English-translated Bible.

Perhaps the cruellest twist of this story is that in 1534 Henry VIII broke with Rome and set up the Church of England, whose new Archbishop of Canterbury, Thomas Cranmer, ruled in 1539 that every church in England should have an English-translated Bible.

*Now there is a slate plaque near the site of the burnings, and a display in the local museum, but it seems nature, and the supernatural, have their own way of marking this tragedy. It is said that no crops grow on the site of the pyres, and that the Chequers Inn is haunted by the sounds of shrieking and screaming, which many believe are the tormented souls of Joan Clerke and the seven Amersham martyrs.*

## DENIZENS OF ANOTHER WORLD

*We tend to think of UFOs as being a modern phenomenon, yet H.G. Wells wrote his science-fiction classic* The War of the Worlds *in 1897. This story from High Wycombe is supposed to have happened in 1871. Perhaps H.G. Wells had been inspired by a truth stranger than fiction.*

William Loosley was a local builder and undertaker who lived on Oxford Road and he knew when life needed to be taken seriously. A good member of the community, he went about his daily routine with little to mark it as remarkable. One day all his hard work caught up with him, and he was taken to bed with a fever. Just after midnight, burning up and sleepless, he got up and went out into his garden for some air.

It was there looking over to Plomer Hill that he noticed a star moving strangely in the heavens. At first, he thought it a falling star, but as he watched its slow deliberate wanderings as though searching he realised it was 'no mere falling star'. He watched as the 'steady, unearthly white' light slowly settled on Plummers Green. Although he watched for a while longer, no more seemed to occur, so he returned to his bed.

Feeling better the next day, he dressed and set out across Littleworth to the place where he had seen the strange glowing object land. As he searched, a movement in the bushes caught his attention, so he poked into the under-growth with a stick. Suddenly there was a loud 'Clank!' as his stick struck metal. When he pulled the briers away there was a metal-cased craft moving with 'whirrings and lurchings. The white globe hung in the air and hoops with globes at their centre which appeared and disappeared.'

Taken aback, and never having seen anything like this before William exclaimed: 'Sirs, your conjure show is all a mystery to me!' and after some time spent in wonderment, he let the craft be and returned home. He later reported his encounter in *An Account of a Meeting with Denizens of Another World.*

## BULL RIDERS

*'When William conquered English ground,*
*Bulstrode had a year three hundred pound'*
*(Old Bucks Rhyme)*

In 1066, William the Bastard conquered England, and in gratitude to his followers he took the manors and estates of the Anglo-Saxon nobles and gave them to his newly appointed Lords. One of these new lords had been granted an area of what is now Bulstrode Park, just west of Gerrards Cross Common, and he eagerly set out to take up his new estate. When he got there, he found that the Saxon Lord, Shobbington, had armed his considerable number of serv-ants and tenants; he was in no mood for simply handing over the estate.

Humiliated, the Norman lord had to return to King William and beseech him for help. The King did not suffer fools gladly, but he suffered nonsense from these Anglo-Saxon fools even less gladly. So the King gave the Lord 1,000 men to oust the wayward Shobbington and hoped that would be the last he would hear about it.

However, Shobbington was a popular man and had friends and allies still at court. They warned him of the coming trouble. This gave Shobbington enough time to call to arms his Anglo-Saxon noble allies, the Penns and the Hampdens who, with their servants and tenants, quickly came to Shobbington's aid. They set to work constructing a mighty earthwork that encompassed twenty-one acres of land; inside they had food, water and grazing cattle, enough defences to hold off the Normans, and enough supplies to wait out any siege.

Which was just as well because that is exactly what the Normans did. Arriving to find the Anglo-Saxon entrenched behind that vast earthwork, the Norman Lord – knowing he couldn't return to the King empty handed again – ordered that no one should be allowed in or out of the defences.

One thousand soldiers might sound a lot, but when they had to guard such a large area day and night, it simply wasn't possible for them to stop the Anglo-Saxons coming and going virtually at their ease.

This stalemate continued for days, stretching into weeks, all the time the Norman lord becoming even more of a laughing stock for his men and peers. Both sides occasionally tried to catch the other one out and skirmishes would ensue until finally Shobbington had had enough. He decided that it was those Normans that had to go, and so they drew up battle plans for the final fight.

The trouble was that the Anglo-Saxons simply didn't have enough horses and knew that the Norman cavalry would be their undoing. Going for a walk around his enclosure, Shobbington looked out across the fields and saw his herd of bulls grazing, and an idea just crazy enough to work sprang to mind. He ran back to camp and ordered the saddles to be brought, and on the morning of the battle, whilst the Penns and Hampdens rode out on horseback, Shobbington and his seven sons rode out astride the backs of bulls.

Seeing the enraged beasts of burden charging soon broke the Norman line, and chaos in the ranks ensued. It was not long before the intruders had been chased from the field and Shobbington's forces were victorious.

The news of this strange encounter did not take long to reach William the Conqueror's ears and he commanded the Norman lord and Shobbington to come to court and explain themselves.

The Norman lord came shamedfaced to court at Windsor, where William sat waiting to hear an explanation, thusly reprimanding his knight for his cowardice. However, the proceedings were soon in complete disarray as riding into court came Shobbington and his sons on their strange mounts and, upon seeing this startling sight, King William was both aghast and impressed. Yet, never one to lose the upper hand, when Shobbington and his sons came before the King, William demanded: 'How dare you resist when the rest of the kingdom has submitted to my government?'

Shobbington replied with dignified respect: 'I and my ancestors have long enjoyed that estate. I did nothing more than protect my own. As your Highness protected his claim to this throne. If your Highness would permit me to retain my lands, I will become your faithful subject.'

King William was impressed again, and stripped the Norman lord of his glory and indeed secured the rights over the estate to Shobbington and his heirs thereafter, giving them and their lands the new title of Bulstrode.

# DON'T EAT THE STEW!

*On the Buckinghamshire border sits Colnbrook, which these days falls under the unitary authority of Slough, although its historic boundaries lie in Buckinghamshire. This village upon the Coln brook has a dark history that gave the brook and the village its name.*

In the reign of Henry I of England, there lived six wealthy, notable, and worthy clothiers in the west, and King Henry himself named Thomas Cole of Reading one of the most famous. These six clothiers would meet in Basingstoke and travel to London together, for the road was treacherous with bandits and cut-throats.

These well-respected tailors would lead a great caravan of carts to the London markets, and by the time the day was done, their pockets would be overflowing with coins. At market they would meet with the great clothiers of the north and together, as there is safety in numbers, they would start their journey by heading north and crossing the dreaded heath of Hounslow. The travellers would breathe a great sigh of relief once they were across, and waiting for them like a glittering oasis in the gathering gloom was the Ostrich Inn, or maybe it was the Crane Inn, it was hard to tell by the painted sign.

The clothiers knew they would receive a hearty welcome, for the landlord Thomas Jarman and his wife always saw to it that when the wealthy tailors arrived, many of the local women from the nearby village were on hand to serve and entertain the gentlemen in every respect.

Thomas Cole of Reading booked into his room and, as he always did, handed over his day's takings to the hostess for safe keeping. Indeed, everyone did so because over the years they had learnt to regard the friendly landlord Jarman and his wife like trusted friends. Thomas always felt a great sympathy for the poor landlord. When getting up in the morning, they noticed a guest missing.

'They nicked out in the night without paying,' muttered Jarman, frustrated at his loss. Often the wealthy clothiers would give the humble landlord an extra coin or two to help recover his loss.

Well as it happened, on one occasion Thomas Cole found it necessary to travel alone, and whilst the day had profited him well, Thomas could not shake a feeling of dread that only increased as the day went on. He was in need of a friendly face and so he decided to stop for the night at the Ostrich. He arrived as darkness fell upon the small hamlet, but first he stabled his horse.

As usual, the Jarmans gave him a hearty welcome, they were discussing if their prize pig was styed for the night, and Jarman said, 'aye, in the top sty'. Thomas handed over his day's takings for safe guarding and, seeing that he was in a melancholic mood, his hostess arranged to give Thomas the best room in the house, the Blue Room.

He sat by the fire and ate a stout meal, yet still the foreboding weighed heavy upon him until he decided that he would write his will, in case some terrible thing was to happen to him. There in the tavern he wrote his last will and testament, leaving all his worldly goods and wealth to his wife Eleanor and daughter Isobel, and £200 for his good friend Thomas Dove – another notable clothier who had fallen on bad times. Landlord Jarman and his good wife witnessed the will and suggested they kept it safe overnight, but a messenger lad was there, and so Thomas Cole dispatched the will straight away.

Feeling a little better that if the worst should happen his family would be taken care of, he retired to his room. As he lay in the gloom a screech owl flew past the window, calling out such a clamour it would wake the dead; a bad omen, thought Thomas, but he tried not to think on it and get some sleep. As he was nearly in sleep a night raven, black as midnight, tapped upon his window pane, rapping a raucous rhythm; another terrible omen, but Thomas tried to put it from his mind and finally a deep sleep took him.

Directly below the Blue Room, the tavern kitchen was ablaze as Jarman stoked a huge fire beneath the large stew pot filled with bubbling water. As his wife came in, Jarman looked up from his work and asked: 'Has the prize pig bedded down for the night?'

'Aye,' said his wife, 'all is quiet without.'

With that, Jarman reached up to the ceiling and pulled on two iron pins, which loosed a great trapdoor that swung open and the sleeping Thomas Cole was sent tumbling from his bed into the boiling water below, where he was drowned and scalded to death.

The noise caused such a din that it startled Thomas' horse, which bolted from the stables and ran to a nearby field where a stud mare was kept. The farmer rushed to protect his investment and called his son to find out whose horse had intruded. The boy recognised it as belonging to one of those fancy clothiers who stay at the Ostrich. So the farmer told the lad to take it back and get well compensated for the trouble.

The lad arrived and banged on the door. The Jarmans took fright, thinking the game was up and in a fit to hide the evidence, for Thomas was not yet cooked down, they emptied out the water and the body into the brook, and then escaped away to Windsor Forest, where they were found and arrested and confessed all. Their lust for wealth had led them not just to steal, but to murder too; sixty bloody murders they owned up to, so they were tried, convicted and hanged.

And now you know how the village got its name.

# THE RAVEN'S CURSE

*The next story wanders a little outside the county's borders to West Drayton, but in the past the county was bigger. The old histories and records hold this story to be from Buckinghamshire, and therefore it is included here as part of the rich tapestry of the heritage of the county.*

Once there was a husband who loved his wife very much and would do anything for her, she only had to ask. They both came from good families and their match had been well celebrated locally. So, when the husband found out that his wife had betrayed him for another man, it broke his heart and sent him quite mad.

In a jealous rage he murdered his young and beautiful wife, and knowing that he could not live without her he took his own life. It was a tragic story and so the families decided to try to petition for the couple to be united in death as they couldn't be in life. So instead of the husband, a murderer and suicide case, being buried in a pit with a stake through his body at the crossroads near Harmondsworth, he was instead interred in consecrated ground. Both victim and murderer were placed in the vaults under West Drayton Church so that he could be laid next to his beloved but unfaithful wife for eternity.

That is when the strangest things began to occur. The sexton of the church – normally a very sensible and pious man, utterly 'devoid of superstition' – began to hear strange noises, knocking sounds, and things falling over without being touched, all coming from the vault under the chancel. It quite disturbed him, but things only got worse. Soon a large black raven appeared in the vault pecking at the lid of the murderer's coffin. Later it was seen pecking at the grating and fluttering around inside the vault, and it even haunted the graveyard, shrieking and screaming at passers-by.

One night, the bell-ringers came to find a lad running towards them saying that the bird was flying around the chancel. Sure enough, there it was flapping about in the rafters. So, the four men and two boys went to gather tools, sticks and stones and lanterns to drive the bird out. They hollered at it, they shook sticks in the air, they threw the stones up into the rafters, and still the bird continued to flap around. As the bird flew back and forth, the men became more and more agitated, beating the bird with sticks whenever they could until its wing was broken. It fluttered down screaming and the men in that instant seized upon it, but it vanished in a moment.

Over the years since, the fluttering of wings and even the raven itself has been seen numerous times, still screeching and screaming. They say that ravens carry the souls from this life to the next and even have the power to bring them back, so maybe the screams of a husband's torments confess his sins, or maybe it is his eternal heartbreak.

# 2

# STORIES FROM NORTH BUCKINGHAMSHIRE

## DR ALLEN'S FAMILIAR

*As far back as 1275, mechanical clocks have satisfied our eagerness to keep track of time, the first one being invented in England. Most early clocks were set upon churches and told the time not with hands and numerals but by chiming out the hours. They didn't all tell the same time either. To set the clock you would need to know what the time was, which you set from the sun (not an exact art) or another clock, so a rider would be sent out to the next village to enquire the time, say it was 11 o'clock, they would then ride back to their own village and inform the clock setter it was 11 o'clock … but what about the time it took to ride? This is why the pocket watch was a very useful invention. The earliest pocket watch was created in 1574 but did not become popular until the late 1660s when Charles II made waistcoats fashionable. Therefore, there were about a hundred years where pocket watches were so rare as to be objects of awe and wonder.*

Dr Allen was so good and so skilled that many believed him to be a wizard. So, when he came to stay at a house in Thornton his reputation had already preceded him, and the maids of the household were slightly afraid.

The year was 1630, and watches were a rare sight. So, when the chambermaid was sent to Dr Allen's room to tidy it, she became quite terrified when she saw the strange ticking object moving of its own accord beside the doctor's bed.

She became convinced that this was his familiar, given to him by the devil itself, and she could not abide such a thing to be in the house. Afraid to pick it up with her hands, she went to the fireplace and, using the fire tongs, took hold of the timepiece and flung it from the window into the moat outside in order to 'drown the devil'.

But as the old saying goes, as 'one who is born to be hanged cannot be drowned', the timepiece survived. Dr Allen returned to his room and, finding the pocket watch missing, he searched high and low. Upon peering out of the window, he saw it hanging on one of the bushes on the bank of the moat. He duly went outside, collected it and placed it back in his pocket.

Later that day, as the chambermaid was helping serve dinner, Dr Allen took the timepiece from his pocket, whereupon the girl nearly fainted seeing the watch had survived. This only confirmed her suspicions and she wouldn't go near the mechanised monster or Dr Allen for the rest of his stay.

## THE EARL'S FOX

*Hunting is something that most people these days feel is cruel and outdated (with good reason). However, hunting once made up a large part of the countryside calendar and social gatherings, but stories like this next one show that even when it was common practice, there were those who rejoiced in the undoing or usurping of the hunt.*

One morning, the blacksmith was called early to the earl's house for his horses needed shoeing. So the blacksmith set off with his tools, but he found on the road a poor fox looking so bedraggled that the blacksmith stopped in his tracks. The poor wretch's ears lay flat to his head, and he held up a paw that, even across the distance, the blacksmith could see was swollen.

Talking in the hushed calm voice he used on horses, the blacksmith moved forward and examined the swollen paw. Using a horseshoe nail, he dug out a sharp object. The fox instantly showed much relief and bolted through the hedgerow, giving one last look at the blacksmith, who carried on his way.

The next morning the blacksmith was up early and heading out to work when he opened his front door and blow me down if there weren't two fat fowls dead on his doorstep. No sign of who might have left them, but the blacksmith had a mind to who it might be. The next day there were two ducks, and the following day a fat goose. This went on for many days, until one morning the doorstep was empty. Perhaps the debt is paid, thought the blacksmith, and he set off to his work.

As he came down the lane, the same fox dashed past him up towards the manor house, followed soon after by a wheezing and puffing farmer.

'Ave you seen a devil in a red fur coat? I'm out to get 'im. These past few weeks he has cleaned me out of hen, duck and goose!'

The blacksmith, trying hard to look as innocent as possible, told the farmer he saw him heading in to the woods, and, with a 'Tally Ho!' the puffing farmer was off again. The blacksmith made a note to knock a bit off the farmer's next bill.

Now the fox, still running for his life, dashed into the great house and straight into the earl's own study, where he was sat by the fire smoking a pipe and reading the morning paper. The fox leapt into the seat opposite and took up a second pipe 'as natural as any gentleman'. The earl looked on in surprise and called to his manservant.

'James! Do you see this?'

'Aye m'Lord.'

'What the devil do you make of it?'

'Perhaps he ran out of tobacco at home, m'Lord.'

Next, the fox took up the discarded newspaper and started to read, and the stunned earl cried, 'James! Do you see this? What does he want with the paper?'

'Well, m'Lord, how else will he know where and when the hounds and hunt meet if he doesn't read the paper?'

'What an extraordinary creature!' the earl mused, 'and it gives me quite the idea for a plan. Whilst I enjoy the hunt for the chase, the exercise and the fresh air, I have never had the stomach for the last bit – you know, the killing part. This fox is of such exceptional intelligence. Therefore, Mr Fox, I have an offer for you: if you will run the hunt, I promise no harm will come to you, and you will be rewarded with a coop of fat hens for your trouble. What say you?'

The fox put down the paper and eyed the earl, and then taking the pipe from his mouth nodded, leapt down from the chair and off he went out of the study, and back to the fields, making sure to avoid the still searching and wheezing farmer.

A week later, a hunt was called across Aylesbury Vale, and the earl came carrying an ornate box. For three hours the hunt searched for fox or hare, but none were to be found, it was as though they had all been forewarned and left the area for the day. Only when frustration was rife did the earl reveal his secret and let the cat out the bag ... or in this case the fox out the box. The dogs yapped loudly and Mr Fox for a moment seemed to cower, but the earl whispered his solemn promise that Mr Fox would be safe, and so out of the box he dashed, followed moments after by the hounds, horses and cries of 'Tally Ho!'

Now, Mr Fox was cunning already, but over the past week the earl had schooled him in the way of the hunt. A plan was set to stick close to the rails, but avoid the brooks, to cut through hedges good for the jumps, and fences when he could. For a while the hunt was enjoyed by all, with Mr Fox outsmarting the dogs and the horses thundering about the countryside. But then Baron Rothschild grew tired of the day and set loose five great hounds, whose speed and ferociousness was nigh on supernatural.

They chased Mr Fox down and the game was nearly up, so our red-furred hero went to ground. Then the rest of the hunt on heavy hooved horses caught up; the hounds and hunters searched and dug to find their quarry. All, that is, except for the earl and his servant James, who went round the other side of the dell and gave a whistle. A few moments later a very weary looking Mr Fox poked its head from the bushes and hopped into the box.

Soon the earl, James and Mr Fox were back home enjoying a pipe, a fire, and a good cup of tea.

## WINGRAVE WITCHES

*Between 1643 and 1661 the persecution of alleged witches was rife. Anybody could be called a witch; men and women alike were interrogated by witchfinders – the men charged with hunting out those in league with the devil – or faced the wrath of the local mob. The lonely, the old, the pet lovers, the disabled, the unsociable or the disliked were often the accused. Fallen out with someone in the village and then had a spot of bad luck? Obviously, the person you fell out with is a witch. Get them! If the accused was discovered to be a witch, often the accuser stood to inherit parts of the money, lands, or goods owned by the witch.*

*By 1726, statutes against witchcraft were repealed, and whilst the witchfinders were out of a job, people were still being arrested and even hanged for being a witch. Yet, fear can do strange things and live on for a long time, so often those suspected of being a witch were dealt with harshly by their own communities and even the authorities.*

*As you can imagine, many were accused and suffered horribly, often subjected to torture in order to gain a confession. If found guilty they were hanged and then their bodies burnt. There were only a few instances where people were burnt alive at the stake, except in Scotland where it was the popular way to dispatch a witch. Yet, talking of Scotland, that is where we must go to understand why the witch trials happened.*

In Berwick the witches are famous because King James
VI of Scotland (later James I of England) was sailing with
his wife back to Edinburgh when suddenly the calm seas
became stormy, and lighting flashed all around, setting the
very water alight as thunder rolled with ominous intent. The
king himself said he saw many witches row out in sieves and
paddle around the ship anticlockwise chanting some foul
spell. The wind roared and the sea churned, and the ship was
tumbled this way and that, until it very nearly broke in half.
The king's wife took up her Bible and began to read aloud,
and so affronted by the sound were the crones, they sailed
off, leaving the king's ship to make it safely to harbour. This
encounter so terrified the young king that when he became
King of England, he brought his fear of witches with him
and his story, so people from city to cowshed knew it, even
in Wingrave …

In that small village lived an old woman called Susanna
Hannokes. To while away her days, Susanna liked to spin wool,
and one day she ran out of flax and went to her neighbour
for some. But Susanna was old and gnarled
and alone, and the neighbour hurriedly
closed her door against the old woman.
Susanna returned home and
lit a fire to stave off the cold.

Meanwhile, the neigh-
bour sat down at her
own spinning wheel and
made ready to begin
her work but, try as she
might, the wheel would not
turn. It had been fine earlier,
and now it would not work.
By the time the neighbour's
husband arrived home

from the fields his wife was besides herself, convinced that Susanna had bewitched the spinning wheel. What were they to do? What other terrible things might occur now the witch had turned her evil eye on them? Did that milk taste sour? Was their cow limping? Did the dog just speak? The wife wept and worried, her husband furious but fearful. As he looked across, he saw a light still burning and the chimney still billowing out smoke from Susanna's cottage. What if she was entertaining the devil at that very moment? The man thought something should be done but was far too afraid to go over to a witch's house in the dark. He had heard the stories. There was no telling what an angry witch and the devil might do if confronted. There was really only one thing to do, and that was to report it! But maybe in the morning when the sun was up.

So, the following morning the husband took his case to the magistrate, who listened – but the statutes had been repealed, and surely if the devil was involved it was a job for the Church? Besides, thought the magistrate, who wants to get on the wrong side of a witch? So, the husband visited Reverend William Wooley, a devout man, a man secure in his faith.

The husband tells his tale of the bewitched spinning wheel and the terror of living next to a witch, and oh what would become of their mortal souls. Upon hearing the story, Reverend Wooley agreed that the husband was right to bring this to him. As the Bible says, 'thou shall not suffer a witch to live'. Reverend Wooley knew that it was their duty to root her out and put her through trial by ordeal.

The husband and some friends fell upon Susanna's cottage; they burst in and the old woman was dragged through the streets to the church. The poor old woman wailed and struggled, but her frail frame was overcome by the mob, who blocked their ears against her cries for fear that she would curse them. Onlookers soon followed, until a crowd was gathered at the church where Reverend Wooley addressed them, as calmly as if he were giving a Sunday service:

'Good people of Wingrave, this woman known to you as Susanna Hannokes, is accused of witchcraft and cavorting with the devil. She cursed her neighbour's spinning wheel to stop it spinning, so she is brought before you now to undergo trial by ordeal. Her body will be weighed against the church Bible and, should she be a witch, her body being governed by unnatural powers will be lighter. Bring her.'

People knew that for the trial to be done properly the witch must be stripped of her clothes in case they had weights in them to make her heavier. Suddenly hands were upon her, pulling at her clothes, tearing and ripping until the old woman stood in the church, cold and naked. After she had been examined for a witch's mark she was brought to a large set of scales. The Bible was place on one side, and Susanna roughly pushed onto the other side. The church went silent as the Reverend and crowd looked on as the scales swung suddenly downwards on one side. In the stillness of that church there was no denying the result. Susanna was definitely heavier than the church Bible (which were mighty tomes in those days). The crowd quickly dispersed, no one daring to look Susanna in the eye. She was left to gather her clothes and make her way home. Susanna was one of the lucky ones, for if she had been found guilty, she would have been ducked and usually that meant being drowned. So maybe the Reverend Wooley had known she would outweigh the Bible and that the trial was more likely to acquit her in the eyes of his parishioners. Or maybe he believed the story and was carrying out his religious duties. Towns can be incredibly small places when rumours abound, and until the end of their days some would always suspect old mother Hannokes of being a witch, despite the result of the trial. So just remember, always greet her kindly, but never look her in the eyes.

# THE WITCH'S HURDLE

*In the heart of the county lay three villages close by one another and forming a triangle: Bishopstone, Stone, and Eythrope. Much like the Bermuda Triangle, this Buckinghamshire Triangle holds many a strange tale too. When H. Harman visited a Bishopstone taproom (pub) one summer's evening he joined the conversation of three regulars and soon heard about the strange and mysterious tales of witches as handed down to them from their fathers, all save for the old watchman, who had a tale of his own …*

A very long time ago in the small village of Bishopstone, there lived a witch. Some said she was wicked, and some said she was kind, but all agreed she had a powerful magic. When she was already wizened and crone-like, the witch gave birth to a bonnie baby boy, who grew and grew and grew. By the time he was a young lad he was immense and incredibly strong, but what he had in muscles he lacked in brains, and the old witch was always chasing after him for one calamity or another.

One day, to ensure that her son didn't get into any misadventure, she told him that he was to come with her as they went to the meadow that day. She sat him down in the corner of the meadow and told him to sit still and whatever he did and whatever he saw, he must stay quiet. 'Can you remember that, boy?'

'Aye, mother, I'll do just as you say.'

And with that the witch left him be and went about her business.

First, she gathered herbs and wildflowers, and when that was done, seeing that her great love, her son, was dozing in the sun, the old witch went over to where one of the sheep hurdles lay. She picked it up, shook it and under the breath of her magic chant the hurdle suddenly came to life and galloped around the meadow with the old witch sitting on it.

The sound of the galloping hurdle awoke the sleeping son; he got up from his makeshift grass bed to see his mother galloping here and there, all over the meadow. As he watched, his mother headed towards the brook at the far side of the meadow, where rider and hurdle jumped neatly across. The lad was so delighted by these antics that he clapped his hands together and shouted, 'Well jumped, mother!'

The instant the sound sprang from his clapping hands and open mouth, the hurdle stopped still and returned to its wooden state. The old witch was sent flying head over heels until she landed with a bump in a cluster of nettles. As she got herself up, the witch was in such a rage that her son was lucky he didn't instantly become a toad from her stare alone. She marched across the field shouting and pulling at her hair: 'When I be doing such things as these, you mustn't speak, for when you do the spell is broken.' She clouted him around the ear and said, 'Don't you know anything boy? More muscles than brains.' They both went home for their supper in a sorry state, and the boy said not a word.

So, be warned, 'those ole witches would get a hurdle and go halfway round the world and back in ten minutes, nobody never knew what they could do.'

# A STARE AS HARD AS STONE

*It was thought that the only way to stop a witch bewitching cattle was to 'blood' them (to make them bleed in some way).*

The carter was heading towards the little village of Stone, and already he was geeing up his team of four horses to get up Eythrope Hill. The horses struggled with their load but once they reached the top, the carter called to his team: 'That's it lads, it's an easier road now.'

On the crest of the hill a few cottages crowded together, and as the tired horses came near these buildings, they stopped dead in their traces and began to shiver and shake like the leaves of a tree on a stormy day. No matter how much the carter called out encouragement, shook the reins, or even snapped the whip those horses would not move an inch. Jumping down from his seat, the carter examined his beasts, whose wild eyes and flaring nostrils told him that they had been spooked by something.

Looking around, he saw an old woman watching them from the front gate of one of the cottages. At first, he paid it no mind, thinking that his beasts were making a right show of him. But he looked again at the way the woman was looking intently with an unblinking, unwavering, cold and callous stare. Something told him that things weren't quite right. There was a chill on the air when it had been warm but a moment ago. The birds had stopped singing, and he felt an unpleasant pressure pushing down on him. Then he remembered the story he'd heard in the public house that witches lived around these parts, and that the one in Stone was the most unpleasant of the lot.

He realised she was bewitching his horses and putting a terrible fright upon them. A sudden fear began to coil its way around his chest like a serpent and he knew that he and his team of horses had to leave that place and quickly. He dashed over to the old crone and with his whip lashed at her hand. She howled out as the blood flowed and the stare and the spell were broken.

The carter leapt into the cart for now the horses were free, and they sprang back to life, causing the cart to speed away as fast as that team of horses could run before the old hag could wreak her revenge. Never during the rest of his days did the carter pass by those cottages ever again.

## The Little Witches

*In Eythrope they have stories of 'little witches' that seem to describe fey (fairy) folk rather than wizened old crones that we see in other stories.*

One evening, the night watchman at Eythrope House went to visit his friends in the Bishopstone taproom. There they got to talking about witches.

'Well, my old father, he used to tell us tales of witches; folk don't seem to see 'em now, but this is what my ole man told me …

'This land is ancient and whilst it has been worked by man and beast for generations, those who spend weeks and sometimes months living outdoors in harmony with the land know that man and beast are not the only things that call these wild places home.

'One evening, after an old shepherd had gathered up his flock, he was calling to his dogs when he turned around to look up to his sheepfold, when he noticed that all the sheep was staring in the same direction. He followed their gaze, and there he could see a strange little man on the top bar of the hurdle. The shepherd knew at once that it was one of the little witches, with its body like a balloon, long dangly legs and a peaked nose. The wee fellow was pulling all manner of faces at the sheep, some which seemed impossible caricatures to contort a face into, and the sheep could not take their eyes from him.

'The shepherd carefully approached the little figure, who instantly stopped pulling faces and shouted, "Hippy, hippy! Over the hedge I go," and riding the hurdle like the wind, off galloped the little witch. The sheep returned to grazing and the shepherd didn't see the strange little man for some time. Yet, every so often when he went to lock up the sheepfold there stood the little witch again pulling such strange faces, and every time the shepherd approached the wee little man he would gallop off on the hurdle.'

The watchman sipped his pint and then turned to his eager audience and said: 'I aint seen 'em little fellows in the fields, but being a night watchman, I has seen some odd things up at the big house.' And with another sip he began.

'Well, every night at midnight til when the church chimed one, I has to be at the pavilion in the grounds of the house, for it be by that way that the poachers come. So, I and my dog, we waits there you see, standing in the shadows of the laurels so as not to be seen.

'Well this one night, we are waiting as usual when I hears a rustling of leaves and the dog, he pricks up his ears and his nose aint half sniffing about. I thinks to me-self, right boy here those buggers come, we'll get them. So, I holds me breath so not to make a sound until they are close by, only the damn dog starts growling and pulling, and nowt I do calms him. I think our game is up anyway, so I let him pull me from the shadows and there what do I see but a bunch of little fellows, little witches you called 'em. There they were not as half tall as my walking stick and their heads too big for the rest of themselves, and those peaked noses on long faces, which they pulled every which way. Knock-kneed little fellows with short thighs and long shanks, all in short jackets dancing in the moonlight.

'I was right there, a big-un like me-self towering over them, but they didn't care a whistle as they danced, jumped and capered about pulling those odd faces all the while. Like those sheep of yours, I couldn't keep me eyes off 'em. I stood there watching, me dog too, until the chime of that there old church bell rang out one in the morning, and something in that holy sound woke me up from my watching, and I turned away leaving them to their revelries. I tell you, if any poachers had come that way that night they'd have been in as much as a state as I.

'From that night on, I sees 'em quite often, leaping and prancing around, they never do mind my glare and pay no heed to the dog. Strange little fellows I tell you, but up to no harm, jest enjoying themselves, I reckon.'

## WENDOVER WITCHES

*Witches also crop up in Wendover, but this time they are out to cause mischief.*

Wendover was to have a new church, so they raised the funds, gathered the materials, the site was prepared, and work was begun. But that night, as the weary builders enjoyed their suppers and their slumbers, a great cackling could be heard overhead.

Those brave enough to reach their curtains and peer out of their windows saw something to chill them to the bone, for witches were gathered around the site of the new church. The hags collected up all the materials and carried them away and deposited them in a different field. With their deed done, they disappeared off into the night.

When word got around the next day, all the village people were most perplexed, but they weren't going to let a few witches get away with it, so they gathered up the materials and they tried again to build their church.

That night, the witches returned (cackles and all), and once again collected up all the materials for the church and dumped it in their preferred field.

What were the people of Wendover to do? Priests were called, officials were questioned, and no one quite knew what to do. It seemed that each time they tried to move the materials the witches just came back and moved them again. They even made one brave soul remain all night to protect the materials, but when the witches returned, they tormented him so much that the poor fellow ran away home.

This went on until eventually the brave decision was made to build the church exactly where the witches had placed the building materials. This ended the nightly terrors, although for a long time afterwards the field where the church was intended to be built was called Witchall Meadow.


## STOWE-AWAY CHURCH

*The church at Stowe had a troublesome start, for like some of the other churches in this county it seemed that the place where priest and local official planned to build it was not acceptable to more unearthly powers.*

The day the church was started was a joyous one for the people of Stowe, and whilst it is true that the Lord Temple of Stowe House didn't much care for its intended location, the people and Church authorities had already made their plans and work had begun.

But, on the morning of the second day, there was considerable confusion, for when the builders arrived at the foundations of the church they'd built the previous day the foundations had gone.

After much searching, they found that their handiwork had appeared in another field, so they gathered it all up and took it back to the place that was set to be the churchyard.

However, the next morning the church foundations had disappeared once again and reappeared in the other field. For eight days and nights this went on, the church being built during the day only to be shifted at night and then gathered up in the morning and rebuilt during the day.

Even the builders themselves found this constant rebuilding somewhat tiresome. Something clearly had to be done. So, they set a stout but foolhardy fellow – for in truth nobody else wanted the job – to sit night-watch, and he indeed sat there all night guarding the materials, but when the builders returned in the morning, they found their night-watchman a gibbering wreck and the church had disappeared once again.

The poor watchman's jabbering and gabbling was so incoherent that nobody could make any sense of what had happened. This so perplexed even the most stout-hearted amongst them that it was decided that whomever or whatever was moving the church by night was not going to give up, and so if you can't beat them join them. The church was therefore built upon the place that was chosen by the mystical forces.

## THE QUAINTON THORN

*This story starts a long way away from Buckinghamshire and a very long time ago …*

It was said that Joseph of Arimathea was a wealthy Jewish merchant and the Virgin Mary's uncle. This being the case, when Christ was crucified on the cross it was Joseph himself who organised his burial and took care of his body. After Christ's Ascension, Joseph was commanded by St Philip to go on a pilgrimage and spread the gospel to all those who did not know it. Taking the Holy Grail with him on his pilgrimage, Joseph travelled long and far, spreading the word of the gospel until he reached Glastonbury. Here he hid the Holy Grail in a sacred well and close by he plunged his pilgrims' staff into the ground. Overnight it grew into a hawthorn tree, which blossoms every Easter and Christmas Day. He also set up Glastonbury Abbey and, when he died, six of the noblest kings of England carried him to his grave.

Over the years, several cuttings were taken from this miracle tree, and two of these cuttings found their way to Buckinghamshire, one to Shenley Church End, and one to

Quainton, where it was planted in the rector's garden. It grew and grew and grew until it became a mighty tree itself, just like its parent plant, and when the Quainton thorn burst into bud every Christmas Eve, its coming was awaited and celebrated by the people of Quainton and all the villages around.

This became a time-honoured tradition in Quainton and part of people's festive celebrations, but in 1752 the crowd of locals that gathered in that rector's garden were watching and waiting not just for a miracle but for proof.

A new calendar had been imposed upon Britain by Pope Gregory XIII because the Julian calendar (named after Julius Caesar, who is supposed to have invented it) had been found over the years to be out by one day. So, to correct this, Pope Gregory introduced the Gregorian calendar (which is what we use across the world today).

But it wasn't as easy as just changing from one to the other; in order to adopt the new calendar, eleven days had to be lost for Britain to come in line with the rest of

Europe. So, Wednesday 2 September was to be followed by Thursday 14 September.

Now, people all across the land began to worry that their lives would also be cut short by eleven days, whilst others were fearful that moving the saints' days would also mean that they would pray on the wrong day and therefore their soul would be endangered. The worry and woe of the people up and down the country was terrible. However, the people in Quainton had a solution.

They knew that their Miracle Thorn would know the true date.

That Christmas Eve in 1752, the small church was crammed full as not just the people of Quainton gathered for the Christmas Eve service, but people from miles around had come too. In that cold church lit by candle light the people gathered together were kept warm by their faith and so many other souls.

Once the service was finished, people poured out of the church into the bitter chill and crisp night. Down the street to the rector's garden they marched singing carols, and it was soon bursting with 2,000 people gathered from the neighbourhood and outlying villages watching and waiting to see if the Quainton Thorn would bud. By candle light and lantern light they waited, singing hymns and retelling the nativity story. They waited for the midnight bells to chime, when the tree should bud.

At last, the chimes came and everyone stared at the tree for any sign of blossom, but midnight came and went, and the tree did not bud. The people waited on, they waited until late just to make sure, but no bud was seen and so they declared that the following morning was not truly Christmas, and so they put by their celebrations until eleven days later for no pope nor king nor government on earth can change the order of the heavens.

# SIR JOHN SCHORNE

*If you visit North Marston today, you might not realise it was once famed far and wide, with people making great journeys just to drink the local water. Unfortunately, the once sacred well is now covered over and the gold cup from which thirsty travellers drank is long gone, but the story lives on.*

*Sir John Shorne, Gentlemen born*
*Conjured the devil into a bote (boot)*
*(Old Bucks Rhyme)*

John Schorne (sometimes Shorne) grew up in Monks Risborough; he loved the world around him and was good at water divining. John had a caring and pious nature, so it was no surprise when he set his heart on becoming a vicar and a cleric so that he could tend to people's mind, body and soul. He arrived in North Marston in 1289 to begin his post as their vicar, where he remained until his death in 1314. It was long after he arrived that his ability for healing and water divination came to the attention of his parishioners, and soon his good reputation spread far and wide.

The summer was hot; so hot that the streams and brooks had dried up, the pond and rivers were so low that water could not be collected without dredging up great quantities of mud. What little water remained was stagnant and dirty, the animals in the field were dying, and the people were getting sick. It was the same everywhere. People went about with parched lips, and in the village of North Marston the vicar, John Schorne, watched how his parishioners suffered. Returning to his church, his own throat dry and rasping, he prayed. That is where John was when a group of his parishioners came to find him, in desperation – their cattle dead, and their families surely soon to follow. The people knew

John was kind and wise and hoped he could offer them hope, or maybe a special prayer in their times of woe, but John saw the state of things and the worried look on his neighbours' faces and knew that much more had to be done.

He took up his staff and strode out of the church, quickly followed by the group of villagers. Calling upon God's hand to guide him, John walked around the village, with an ever-increasing crowd of dry-lipped gaunt faces watching him until he came to rest at a place where he drove his staff into the ground.

At first there was nothing to see; the villagers' hearts sank. Then very slowly to start with, a trickle of water pushed its way up through the soil.

'Look!' shouted one villager.

'It's a miracle!' exclaimed another.

John looked at those gathered and said, 'Fetch up your hoes and dig.' Those who had them fetched hoes, spades, and any manner of digging tool; those who didn't simply clawed at the ground with their bare hands as only the thirsty can. Soon water was gushing out of the ground, drenching the diggers, but they cared not for the cool fresh water felt wonderful after so many weeks of thirst. They turned that spot into a well, and for North Marston the drought was ended. However, the miracle did not end there, because no matter how much water was taken from the well it did not dry out, even though the drought continued elsewhere for a long time after. People came from far and wide, and yet the water still flowed. With so many people drinking from the well they soon began to realise that the water itself was special and had the power to heal, not just illness related to thirst but much more 'scorbutic and cutaneous diseases, ague and gout'. 'A glass drunk at night could cure a cold by morning.' They say it could cure toothache and the misery of boys. It could even ward off drowning! It seems the water itself had taken on John's own powers to heal.

It was when winter came and the drought long-since passed that another miracle revealed itself. One morning the village of North Marston woke up to a thick blanket of snow covering the land. After the long months of scorching heat, the natural balance had now swung the other way, and the bitter cold stuck fast to every tree, bush and rooftop, and bit hard into the bones. Every source of water was frozen, much to the delight of the children, who slid about throwing snowballs, as children do and have always done at the first sight of snow.

People ventured slowly out of their houses, making sure roaring fires were set to greet them upon their return, and the day started in earnest. It was as people went to fetch water from the well, taking poles with them expecting to smash the ice in order to fill their buckets, that it was discovered. Even in the bitter conditions the well water was not frozen, and despite the cold winter raging on, no matter how cold it got, the water would not freeze. John came to the well edge, the sacred spring he had found and brought forth with guidance from God, and offered up a prayer in thanks. And, so it is, that the water continues to flow, no matter what the weather from that day to this, and over the centuries pilgrims came from all over the land to pay homage and drink the water from a chained gold cup long after John Schorne had died.

In his lifetime his reputation grew, and many people sought out John Schorne to be healed or to learn wisdom. He became known as Sir John Schorne, to show his importance as a cleric. Whilst most of the pilgrims to visit John were pious, not all of them were so.

The devil himself got to hear about the good John Schorne and decided that he would make a good target to tempt and corrupt. So, the devil set off for North Marston disguised as a stranger with an unpleasant aroma of sulphur about him and a long coat to hide his tail and cloven feet (which he always had difficulty hiding). The devil strolled around, taking in the lay of the land.

Unlike other travellers to the area, he would not go near the sacred well-head to drink from its holy waters. Sir John, being ever observant and therefore wise, noticed this and began to be suspicious. Over the next few days all sorts of mishaps and bad luck seem to plague the people of North Marston. Ladders fell over leaving people stuck up high on roofs and trees, bread burnt, milk turned sour even as it was being squeezed from the cow, and flies seemed to be everywhere.

Soon, everyone got to thinking that there was trouble amongst them. It didn't take long for John to realise that the devil was in their midst, and so it was that Old Scratch revealed himself to John. That wily devil tried to tempt John with all sorts of magics and mysteries; perhaps John would like fortunes to go with his fame, perhaps sweet cakes, or expensive clothes, but John was not a foolish man. In fact, by the power of his faith, John had some tricks of his own, for people who use their minds sincerely often do.

So quick as a flash he thought up a plan to trick Old Scratch and tempt him into a trap. 'You offer me so many things,' said John to the devil, 'but how can all these things be so? Can you conjure anything you want?'

'Of course,' replied the devil. 'I can do anything, apart from enter heaven, but I have been there already. I can give you a castle with a kingdom of your own, I can give you treasure … name it and it's yours.'

John looked thoughtful for a moment, and eyed up the devil, then he spoke: 'If my mortal soul is the price, I want proof before I agree to any deal. If you can do anything then turn yourself into something.'

'Certainly,' cried the devil. 'What would you like me to turn into? A dragon, a mountain, gold?'

John thought fast and took off his boot. 'I want to see you make yourself small enough that you can fit inside this boot!'

The devil laughed. 'Ha, that is easy, you mortals have no imagination!'

In that very instant the devil began to shrink down until he became a tiny replica of himself and then flew up into the air and landed inside the boot.

John gripped the top of the boot tight while he said the Lord's Prayer, which burnt the ears of the devil, who screamed and shrieked from inside the boot. John said it three times, for the Father, the Son, and the Holy Ghost. John kept that old devil in that manner, praying at him three times each day until so tormented was Old Scratch, he pleaded with John to stop and promised that if John let him go, he would never again trouble the people of North Marston. So, John let the devil out of that there boot and as the King of Demons hurried his way back down to hell, John called after him: 'And do remember if you ever come back, I have the other boot.'

You can never trust the devil, so John continued the rest of his days to preach the words of God to his parishioners just in case. From that day to this day, the devil has never ever been seen in North Marston again.

*When John died, pilgrims began to flock to his shrine and so popular did it become by the end of the fifteenth century, that the King ordered John's bones to be moved to St George's Chapel in Windsor. After his death there was a small statue built of John Schorne capturing the devil in a boot, and it was said that it was mechanised so that the devil would pop in and out of the boot. It is said this is what gave rise to the popular 'Jack in a box' toy for children.*

## THE BARD IN BERNWOOD

*Bernwood is said to be named after Bernwulfe, the Great Mercian King of AD 820 and found favour with the Kings of England for generations afterwards. But not all areas are so noble. Grendon Underwood was once called the 'Dirtiest town that ever stood' because it was so muddy, but this didn't stop it inspiring one of the greatest writers in the English Language. Rumours say that Shakespeare, in his days as a wandering player, came to the area and found two sources of inspiration for his plays. He stayed in the Ship Inn in Grendon Underwood, where the beauty of the woodlands could be seen from his window, and it was here that he supposedly wrote part of* A Midsummer Night's Dream*, with the locals in the Ship Inn being his Mechanicals in the play. The constables Dogberry and Verges from* Much Ado About Nothing *are also thought to have come from Grendon Underwood.*

One night, a wandering player came by Grendon Underwood and, down on his luck, he didn't even have enough coin for a tankard in the Ship Inn, let alone a bed for the night, so he made his way to the church and there in its porch he lay his head for the night.

Sometime later, the two village constables passed the church on their rounds and, seeing a lump in the shadow of the church porch, they went to investigate and found a sleeping tramp. Suspicious that he was up to no good, those constables woke him up roughly and were all set to charge him with intent to steal from the poor box.

The poor man promised that this was much ado about nothing, for he was a man of good standing, down on his luck, and weary from the road, who just wanted somewhere to dream on this midsummer night before he went on his way. He said that he had stayed at the Ship before, and with any luck the landlord there would recognise him.

The constables, feeling a little guilty for their roughness, took the stranger to the Ship, where the landlord indeed recognised him as the venerable Mr Shakespeare. The constables and Shakespeare set their troubles aside and there in that inn spent some time together becoming firm friends.

## NIEL SHORTSHIRT

*In some versions of this story his name is Nigel, but since that was a name introduced by the Normans it is unlikely that was the huntsman. Or on the other hand it could be a concocted story by an Anglo-Saxon family who wanted their lands back. Either way, here we use Niel.*

In the days when Bernwood Forest covered most of Buckinghamshire, King Edward the Confessor had a hunting lodge at Brill from where the King and his men would venture out into Bernwood Forest to hunt a monstrous boar, which terrorised the forest and the surrounding area. The boar ravaged man and beast alike, and even killed small children. It was of enormous size and despite some of the best hunters and noblemen going in search of it, the beast continued to rule the royal hunting forest.

It was not just that these many hunters came to slay the beast for the sake of king and country-folk, for the mighty boar, huge and fierce was 'counted the most absolute champion among beasts'. To be a boar slayer held the same awe and prestige as being a dragon slayer in the ancient stories. Great songs would be sung; stories would be told, and the slayer would go down in history. Who would not wish for such glory? So, every nobleman in King Edward's court hoped that they would be the one to fell the beast, for this boar had such an infamous reputation that the one who finally slew it would surely be remembered as a legendary hero.

Yet, no matter the skill of the hunters, nobody seemed to be able to capture this boar, whose body was covered with the scars of spear and arrow that had failed to stop the beast. The King wondered who would rid him of this wretched beast that ran rampant in his forest and scared off all the other game.

Near to the forest edge lived a humble huntsman whose name was Niel, a noted forester; not a nobleman but an honest hardworking man of lowly status. He wore a short tunic that showed everyone he was a poor man, for material was expensive and it was always more important to get food on your table than have a fashionable long shirt.

The village in which he lived, being so close to the forest edge, had suffered the worst of the boar's temper. Farmers had lost their herds and crops, the people were afraid to venture into the forest for foraging mushrooms, berries, and nuts. Even Niel had to think twice before venturing out to hunt, always keeping his wits about him, alert to every sound. The people were miserable, the King was miserable, this boisterous boar had to go.

So one day Niel took up his spear, and arrows, and a spade and entered the forest. He made his way quickly into a place where the boar was not often sighted so that he could get to work. He dug long and he dug hard, he dug until he'd dug all day, and at the end of it there was a deep trench in which he placed poles facing upwards and then with his blade sharpened their ends. He rushed back to the village and asked to borrow a sow from his brother, who was a farmer, and leading the pig to his earthwork, he coaxed the sow into the trench. Leaving food for her to munch happily, Niel filled in the trench opening so that now there was a deep pit, which held the sow, and the sharp poles. He swiftly covered up the opening with branches and leaves.

It was twilight, the right time for the boar to be out foraging, but there was no sign of the beast. Niel waited in his hiding place all night long, his muscles cold and stiff, his eyes tired. Yet still he waited.

At first light, the sow in the pit started to create such a racket as to ring out across the forest; she had obviously run out of food, and was not impressed by her new lodgings and longed to return to her snug sty on the farm.

All this noise soon brought the attention of the boar, who came crashing through the bracken and briars. Niel sprang from his hiding place and notched his arrow. Fleet and swift it flew through the air, finding its mark in the boar's chest. Yet still the beast charged on, Niel loosed another arrow and another, until the boar was just yards away. As it lowered its head ready for the final charge, it ran over the covered pit and downwards it tumbled, landing on the spikes. It groaned a terrible cry, which seemed to make the trees tremble and the clouds quake. Niel came to the edge of the pit. Even in the grave state it was, the mighty beast seemed to fight off death as terribly as if it were a foe in the forest. With his last arrow, Niel fired a well-placed shot and ended the misery for both man and beast.

There fell upon the forest a silence, as though a great hero had passed.

Niel dug out the trench entrance and returned his brother's sow, and then returned to the boar. Knowing he would need proof, he took the great beast's head, and set off for the King's hunting lodge. When he came to the guarded entrance it took a lot of convincing for him to be admitted into the King's presence, but finally he was allowed in and he entered a room where the King sat on an ornate chair surrounded by many of the King's lords and earls all dressed in their fine clothes curious to see what this poor man wanted of the King.

'Sire, I come bearing a gift, which I think may please you.' Niel bowed as he reached into his sack and pulled from it the boar's head, which he presented to the King upon his sword.

The lords and earls could hardly believe their eyes. How could this lowly huntsman have defeated the boar, managing a feat that none of them could? As the King smiled and congratulated Niel, the nobles felt the serpent of jealousy twist in their stomachs.

'Look at his shirt, he is a poor man. Surely there must be some mistake,' cried one Earl.

'Perhaps he is the servant of a nobleman who is the real huntsman, and this serf is trying to steal the glory for himself,' protested another.

Edward the Confessor held up his hand for silence and asked Niel to tell the story of how he defeated the boar. When the telling was finished, the King was satisfied and declared that such a hunter, nobleman or poor, should receive a reward. Niel was asked to stand before the King to receive his honour, but as he did so one noble sneered, 'Niel Short-shirt.'

Such a name calling may seem slight, but it was the same as saying Niel the beggar. In front of all these nobles Niel felt humiliated as he knelt before the King, who smiled.

'Niel Short-shirt it is! For you should never be ashamed of where you have come from. It is to you, great boar slayer of Bernwood Forest, and to your heirs, that I give one hyde of land at Deerhyde, one woodland at Hulewood, and the custody of all Bernwood Forest, which you will hold by this horn as a charter from your King from this day on. Although I shall keep my rights to vert and venison, herb and hunting.'

The King gave Niel an ornate hunting horn made from brown buffalo horn. It was so long Niel had to hold it in both hands. It was wrought with silver work and with a coat of arms upon it to seal the promise and a personal coat of arms for Niel and his descendants.

The King invited Niel to stay and feast, and to tell his story again, for he was now the famous and noble boar slayer.

Niel built a great manor house and called it Borestalle (Boarstall) in honour of the fallen beast who won him such fortune. The horn in time became known as the Boarstall Horn and passed down through the generations to show their status as the King's foresters of Bernwood Forest.

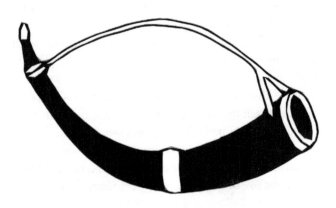

# THE SOULBURY STONE

*If you visit Soulbury as you pass on the 'Buckingham Way' it is highly recommended you take time to visit the cul-de-sac of Chapel Hill, for there you will see in the middle of the road a large boulder. This is the Soulbury Stone, and it proves not all stories have to be old to be a tale of folks.*

Once, a very long time ago, there was a stone. Nobody knew from whence it came but they did know to where it went. They say a rolling stone gathers no moss and maybe that's why it set out on its journey, for this stone rolled and rolled and rolled until one day it stopped. It stayed on the spot where it stopped, not just for a little while, but it so liked the place that it decided it would never be moved.

In time, a small village grew up around it, and people came to be fascinated by this stone, because, without being told, it seemed to represent their own story of how they had made their own home at this very spot. It is said that the people who grew up around the stone had a rock-like determination.

The young bucks of the village tried to show how strong they were by pushing at it but no matter how hard they tried the stone would not budge, whilst others would try to vault it thinking that at only three feet high it seemed such an easy thing to do, especially if you had already had a pint or two down at the Boot public house. But that stone was not going to be conquered by anyone, and somehow it would rise up to meet them in mid-air so that many a young chap would have to be carried home with a damaged undercarriage as he tried to glide over the stone.

The people of Soulbury were rightly proud of their stone and cried out, 'the Soulbury Stone never loses'. But it doesn't always stay still either, because sometimes at Halloween and sometimes on other nights when it has a will to do so, the

Soulbury Stone takes to rolling again. The villagers say the stone rolls down the hill at night but is always back in its usual spot by morning.

The stone stood there and watched whilst Oliver Cromwell stood on top of it and watched as the Parliamentarian troops ransacked the village church, and the people of the village were tormented and investigated for their Royalist sympathies, but the stone and people would not be moved.

Many years later, another war was taking place; the Second World War took many of the Soulbury lads far away to fight on foreign shores and lands. As well as taking the lads, the army thought it would take the stone too. Very official-looking officers looked on as two large tanks trundled up the road and chains were fastened around the boulder, but as hard as the tanks pulled, the Soulbury Stone did not move from its home. So instead they tried to use the tanks to push the stone, but still it stuck fast, and the tanks came off worst. Finally listening to the locals, they let the stone win and left it in its resting place, for the stone and people would not be moved.

When there were plans for London's third airport to be placed upon Soulbury and for the stone to be moved, the villagers protested so loudly to protect their stone; the stone and people would not be moved.

In 2016 the authorities, this time Buckinghamshire County Council, decided that they too would try to take on the stone because an unfortunate lady had reversed her vehicle into it and complained that it was an obstruction. The county council investigated and decided that perhaps it was time that the stone was indeed moved. Yet the locals were so enamoured of their mystical stone that had stayed with them through thick and thin, that they too would choose to stand by their stone, even if that meant chaining themselves to it. Faced with such determination,

Buckinghamshire County Council decided to give up their quest to move the stone, because the stone and people would not be moved.

For, as the locals proudly proclaimed, 'the Soulbury Stone never loses'.


## A Ghostly Guard Dog

*Whilst you're in Soulbury, you might want to keep an eye out for another strange tale, or should that be tail? All across the land, ghostly black dogs have been sighted – usually as a bad omen – and are often linked to the Wild Hunt and Green Men (see the Green Man of Fingest). However, the phantom pooch in Soulbury seems to be much better natured.*

Once a very long time ago there was a farmer and his family who lived in Stewkley. Each week they would travel from their home to the market at Leighton Buzzard and, as they journeyed, they would make their way through the small village of Soulbury. The road they travelled was often fraught with danger, especially for farmers on their way home, their purses heavy with the sale of their wares. Ne'er-do-wells, thieves and outlaws would lurk in bushes and on dark stretches of the road waiting for the next victim to pass by.

One night, passing through Soulbury, the farmer's wife looked down and there running beside the cart, seemingly out of nowhere, appeared a black dog. It kept perfect pace with the cart. At first the farmer and his family all wondered if the dog had wandered off from its owner and they stopped to ask a passer-by, who looking around saw no dog, and didn't know of anyone who had a beast to match that description.

So, the farmer, his family and his cart carried on, and moments later the dog appeared at their side once more. Deciding that it was getting late and they needed to get home, they carried on their way, thinking that they could always bring the dog back when they returned this way the following week.

Just as their home of Stewkley came in sight, the farmer's children, who had been watching the dog, saw it disappear into thin air. The farmer and his family were bemused but they were grateful that they had returned home safely, unlike many others who had travelled that road. The farmer and his family also saw the dog on a number of other occasions as they travelled up and down that road, each time appearing at Soulbury and disappearing just before they arrived in Stewkley. It did seem that the black dog was indeed guarding the family and ensuring their safe passage home.

Over the years, the black dog has appeared to others, most recently a woman visiting Soulbury, who suddenly felt a presence walking beside her and looked down to see a black dog. Being of a friendly nature, the woman bent to stroke its fur but when she reached out her hand to touch its back her hand passed straight through and the dog disappeared.

## THE BLACK DOG

*Another black dog story comes from an undisclosed village near Aylesbury, but this one returns to the normal nature of such haunting hounds and isn't nearly as friendly as the one from Soulbury.*

There was once a farmer who had a herd of cows that he milked every morning and every night. The field in which he kept his cows was a fair distance from the village and, because he had to carry two heavy pails of milk on a yoke across his shoulders, he would often take a short cut across a neighbour's field through a gap in the hedge.

One night, whilst his mind was deep in thought about what he needed to do, the farmer came up to the gap, only to find that a great black dog stood in his way. At first the farmer thought his neighbour had a new dog, perhaps he had offended his neighbour in some way and had put this dog here to block his path and make him walk the long way around.

Yet on a second look, the dog's black fur, which stood up on end, seemed to give off an ethereal glow; its eyes burnt like fire, there was a strong sense of sulphur in the air and as the hound grew larger, the fiercer it got. 'This is no ordinary dog, but a fiendish demon or bad spirit come here to cause trouble,' thought the farmer and, deciding to give it a very wide berth, he turned back swiftly through the gate, intending to go the long way round.

On his return home that night, the farmer dared not take the short cut for fear of meeting the beast in the dark. The farmer hoped that the beast had chosen to cause mischief upon that night only, but the next night there it stood again looking worse than the night before. He tried to tell his neighbour, who insisted he had no new dog, and the ones he had were all accounted for. The neighbour thought the farmer was losing his wits and should waste no more of his time.

But the farmer was not spared and night in and night out the terrible black dog would appear in the pass in the hedge. Even when the farmer no longer took the short cut, he could feel the presence of the hell hound from across the fields.

One evening, as the farmer had just finished milking his cows, a friend from the village walked by and when the farmer started to take the long route, his friend cried, 'Lo, friend, let's be going the short way, and we'll be in the pub all the sooner.'

Afraid, but not wanting to seem cowardly in front of his friend, the farmer agreed to take the short cut. Glancing back, the farmer thought that maybe having someone with him might scare off the strange vision, or perhaps if someone else were to see the beast it would prove he wasn't mad.

Soon they arrived at the gap and there was the black dog, angrier and larger than ever before. The farmer's friend, who had been chatting all the way, suddenly went silent and stared as the dog gnashed its teeth as it guarded that gap in the hedge. The farmer tried to suggest going the other way, but his friend told him not to be cowardly, it was just a dog, just give it a good beating and it will leave. Not wanting to appear faint-hearted in front of his friend, the farmer put down his yoke with the two full buckets, freed the yoke from the pails and swung it like a mighty bat. As the farmer swung, he cried out: 'Now you black fiend, we'll see what you are made of.'

As the yoke struck the place where the dog seemed to be, the dog vanished from sight. In the same moment, the farmer fell senseless to the ground. His friend carried the poor farmer home, bur despite every care the farmer was paralysed and could not speak evermore.

As for the black dog, it hasn't been seen since, but then most sensible folk don't go looking for it.

# ST RUMBOLD

*Twelve miles north of Buckingham, between Brackley and Banbury, is a place called King's Sutton in Northamptonshire and, although it is where this story in part transpires, it ends in Buckingham, and the saint is most closely connected to the ancient town that gave the rest of the county its name.*

*During Roman times, parts of Britain had converted to Christianity when it became the official religion of the empire, but with the exodus of the Roman army and the invasion of the Angles, Saxons, Jutes and Frisians, Paganism returned as the main religion. It wasn't until the seventh century that missionaries visited these shores in earnest to start the difficult job of converting the Anglo-Saxons. At that time the country was divided into several kingdoms, each with its own king or prince. Wessex and Mercia shared a border that ran along the river Ouse in North Buckinghamshire.*

The grand King of Mercia, Penda, was a Pagan and still practiced the old ways, but his daughter, Cyneburga, had heard the Christian missionaries and had converted. Cyneburga was the apple of her father's eye and was quite a beauty, so despite their differences in faith, the King set about finding her a good husband. Mercia's northern border was shared with the kingdom of Northumberland, who could at times be tricky neighbours, but there lived a prince, Alchfrith, who was renowned as handsome, brave and clever. So, King Penda sent word, suggesting the match to the King of Northumberland to broker peace between the two kingdoms.

The King of Northumberland agreed and soon the young would-be lovers were thrown together to meet for the first time. When the pair met, both were charming, both were beautiful, both were clever, and soon they were deep in conversation. Their parents looked on, nodded to the match and started to plan the wedding. But suddenly something went very wrong: Cyneburga got up and left to sit in her room, and refused to come out.

The two kings were dumbfounded and so asked Alchfrith what had happened. He nervously answered that they had been getting on very well, but that she had asked him about Christianity, to which he had replied that he did not think it would catch on.

Penda was enraged; he had gone to great lengths to arrange this match, and now he felt that because of this silly new religion his daughter was risking losing a good husband, and a peace deal. No matter how Penda tried to convince Cyneburga to reconsider, she stayed in her room saying she couldn't marry a man who was not a Christian.

Alchfrith couldn't help but feel a little confused. Cyneburga was all a young prince could want in a wife, and so he asked to meet with her one more time and if she still did not want to marry him, he would leave and never return. She agreed, and they two met, looking shyly at each other. Alchfrith gently apologised for his words and said he knew so little of the new faith, and would she tell him more. And so that afternoon the hours passed as Cyneburga told all that she knew, and Alchfrith listened and sometimes asked questions. By the time it came for the two to part, Cyneburga knew she loved him but that she still could not renounce her faith. Alchfrith knew he loved her too, and so promised he would convert to Christianity, if that was what she wanted. Cyneburga was delighted; Alchfrith was baptised, and soon after there was a grand but pious wedding where Pagan and Christian celebrated together.

The young lovers were the very picture of a royal romance and it was not long before Cyneburga's belly started to swell with the love she shared with Alchfrith.

Penda was worried about his daughter, for in these times childbirth was a dangerous affair. Penda prided himself on having the best healers and told Cyneburga that when the time for the birth was near, they should come to his palace so he could ensure the best care for his daughter and grandchild. The months passed and soon it was time for Cyneburga and Alchfrith to start their journey to Penda's palace.

The road was little more than a broken dirt track – bumpy and full of pit holes. Passing Brackley at a place now called Walton Grounds, near King's Sutton, Cyneburga called out in pain. All that bumping around had caused her labour to begin early, so Alchfrith quickly ordered camp to be made. After a few hours of Cyneburga's cries, and Alchfrith's worry, suddenly a baby's cry called out across that field. Alchfrith rushed to his wife's side, where she held a beautiful baby boy.

The proud parents were at once in love with their child and, like all parents, thought he was the most special and radiant of all babies. Yet this miracle of life became even more miraculous when, in front of his parents and gathered courtiers, the baby spoke. He cried out: 'Christianus Sum, Christianus Sum, Christianus Sum!' (I'm a Christian) and begged to be baptised with the name Rumbold on that very day.

This was a great surprise to all that heard, but his parents with their Christian faith knew it must be a miracle. The problem was that in Anglo-Saxon England at that time, baptismal fonts were hard to come by, for churches were rare. Alchfrith called for his men to search for something that could be used as a font. His men searched high and low, and in a nearby hut they found a stone shaped like a bowl, but it was incredibly heavy, too heavy even for five men to lift. When his men reported this to the prince, little Rumbold told them: 'In the name of the Lord,' fetch the stone and you will find that God will help carry the load. Sure enough, when the men returned the stone seemed to weigh hardly anything and was brought quickly back to the camp, where Rumbold was baptised.

As you can imagine, news spread quickly: not only had a prince been born, but he could talk. Upon the morning of Rumbold's second day, there were gathered a great number of people at the camp. Rumbold asked his mother to carry him out to the crowd and, there lying in her arms, the miracle babe preached a sermon to all who had assembled. He preached on the Christian Virtues and on the Holy Trinity, so that all who heard, whether Pagan or Christian, were in awe of him. That day many a Pagan heart transformed and as the sun set on that camp many new Christians prayed for the first time.

On the third day, the crowd was even bigger, eager to see what miracle would occur that day, but though they waited there was no sign of the babe. Rumbold was laid in his parents' arms, for on the third day he said: 'I was only ever here for a short time, to show you your faith was true, and now I have given my message I must return to God, the father of us all.'

His parents wept bitterly, but the baby reached out his hands and told them not to cry; he had come to them with his miracle and would for ever be part of them. With this, he gave them the solemn instructions for his burial:

'You must bury me for a year in the place where I was born, for this was the place I gave my message. After that, I must be buried for two years in Brackley, from whence my bones must be carried to Buckingham, where I shall rest ever after, and a church is to be built there.'

When his parents promised that all would be done as he had instructed, young Rumbold shared his last few bitter-sweet moments with his mother and father, then his soul rose back to heaven from whence it had come.

With great sorrow in their hearts, but thankful for the blessing they had been given, Cyneburga and Alchfrith did just as they had been told by their miracle son. For a year, he was buried in the field where he was born, then after in Brackley and finally in Buckingham where a church, a shrine and a tomb were built where many pilgrims visited.

*Sadly, the old church in Buckingham collapsed in 1776, destroying the tomb and shrine, and nothing could be saved to be moved to the new church, which now stands on Castle Hill. In Buckingham, St Rumbold's Well can also be found, which is said to cure lameness and blindness. The stone bowl in which Rumbold was baptised is now the baptismal font in King's Sutton church.*

## THE CENTAUR

*Quarrendon was once a small village in Buckinghamshire with a fine house, where Queen Elizabeth I came to stay, but then the village was abandoned and lost, and the fields that now contain its remains are a Scheduled Ancient Monument. Perhaps this medieval ghost-town still has a few secrets to reveal, for over the years people have reported seeing golden yellow fairies about two feet tall dancing in the ruins, and those who watch them are filled with an immense sense of happiness, until the fey folk up and disappear as fey folk have a habit of doing. We think of stories as something that people encountered a long time ago, before we knew about science or mental health issues. But is our modern world so devoid of mystery? Not according to this tale from 1988.*

It was a hot summer evening and the sun showed little sign of setting. So, John and his dog Sheba decided to pay a visit to their friend Richard to enjoy the last of the day's sun, out on the Quarrendon fields by Meadowcroft Road.

It was about 10.15 p.m. and the sun was easing its way down to the horizon, painting the countryside in a beautiful orange glow. Sheba, a well-natured German Shepherd dog, was enjoying running on ahead and investigating the landscape, though she had to wait for her humans to catch up. Richard and John were deep in conversation as they wandered the familiar and well-walked route.

Suddenly Sheba shot passed them, running for home, her ears back and looking terrified. No amount of shouting would call her to stop, which was not like her, as she usually behaved so well. Before heading after her, both men naturally turned towards the place she had run from.

And there it was.

At first neither man could make sense of what they were seeing. The dappled grey hindquarters of a horse, but as it raised itself up there was the unmistakable torso of a man. Not riding the horse but melded into it, where the head of the beast should have been.

In terrified awe, the two men stared at what all logic told them shouldn't be there, couldn't be there. A legendary mythical creature stood in the gathering twilight gloom of the English countryside. It was an impossible situation to comprehend.

As the men regained their senses, the creature held them in its stare. The pair turned and ran for their lives not daring to stop or turn around, the sound of thundering hooves hard behind them, until they reached the road. Glancing back across the field, they were sure they would not still see it, but there it was staring right back at them, then it moved quickly and disappeared into the trees.

When the men arrived back at John's house, they found Sheba waiting for them still shaking with fear. When John's wife asked what had happened, she wouldn't believe them at first but the state of both the men and the dog were enough to convince her. Neither men have ever ventured back to those fields.

## The Last Message

*Be careful as you travel the A418 from Aylesbury to Thame, because as you pass Haddenham you might become another of the unfortunate travellers to have spotted a ghostly figure lingering by the side of the road. Any who see him are cursed with bad luck, but what bad luck brought him to this place?*

There was once a farmer who lived with his wife at Thame, and his name was 'Noble' Edden, so called because a better, more handsome and strong fellow you would never meet. He was a market gardener and cultivated his plants in fields at Crendon that, being on the hill, had far-reaching views all around. One day, he was out working his fields when he spotted two fellows he had seen around Thame. He knew these two ne'er-do-wells by the names of Sewell and Tylor. From his position Noble could see the men but was sure they couldn't see him.

Noble watched as the men entered a neighbouring field, killed a sheep and carried it off. In those days the crime of sheep stealing was a severe one and brought with it the sentence of transportation for life or even the final punishment: to be hanged. Noble knew he should report it, but if he did the death of those two lads would be on his hands, and so he decided to let fate take its course.

The local constable, Seymour, was soon called for as the farmer discovered the missing sheep, but with no evidence the two were never discovered.

Noble found that night he did not sleep, nor the next three nights, as he worried. Even in the public house with his friends as they all drank and chatted, Noble was unusually quiet, afeared that, if he spoke, he might say something about what he saw. However, with a bellyful of ale on his way home from the pub he happened to pass Sewell and Tylor and, before he knew what he was doing, Noble bleated at them. This baited the two villains, who turned to face Noble, but at that moment some of Noble's friends caught up with him. Tylor indicated to Sewell to leave, for now, but once they were alone, they wondered what to do, for now they knew that Noble had seen them.

A few days later, it was Saturday and Noble was up early to go to market in Aylesbury. He had a good day, he had done a good trade and his pockets were full of coin. By the time he packed up his things it was late, and an uncomfortable mood had settled on him. He just couldn't shake the feeling something terrible was in the air, despite having had such a good day.

As he was packing up his wares, he spotted a man he knew from Haddenham and offered the fellow a ride home in his cart. They talked along the way, but Noble couldn't shake a sense of foreboding that had crept upon him the closer he got to home. Noble told his passenger about the strange feeling, and he immediately offered to travel with Noble all the way back to Thame. This seemed to release Noble from his woe and, dropping off his friend, he continued on his way.

Noble was just at Anxey when Sewell and Tylor jumped out of the bushes. They had been waiting for him to make sure he hadn't told anyone else, and they were going to silence him forever. A terrible row broke out and the villains pulled Noble from his cart. The shouting quickly turned to fighting as the men attacked the farmer, who was forced to fight for his life.

Coming down the track, another man heard a terrible noise of fighting, and he was cautiously making his way towards it when a woman, terrified at the noise, appeared on the path and begged to be escorted home for fear of the sounds of bloody murder. And thus, Noble was left to his fate.

At home Noble's wife was ironing, waiting for her husband to arrive home for supper. Feeling an icy chill run down her spine, she looked up from her work and there, where the other side of the room should be, was a vision of a roadside and two men attacking her husband. She watched as Noble, bloody and battered, got to his feet and tried to run, but the man she recognised as Tylor swung a stone breaker's hammer into the back of her husband's head. The vision vanished and the poor shocked woman ran screaming to her neighbours:

'Oh dear God, my husband is being murdered!'

Immediately her neighbours' men set off to search for Noble, while the women tried to comfort Mrs Edden. Yet, search as they might, no sign of Noble was found. Mrs Edden and her son, who believed his mother's vision though he hadn't seen it, were not shy about speaking out against the two attackers. Yet, without a body or proof, nothing could be done.

A few days later a farm hand from Haddenham who was taking horses up to Anxey Meadow found poor Noble's battered body. His body was taken to the cider house in Haddenham to await the inquest a week later. The authorities investigated, but still there was no evidence, apart from Mrs Edden's vision, which was put down to the traumatic grief of a widow. So, a verdict of murder by persons unknown was given, and Mrs Edden was allowed to take home her husband's body, frustrated that Noble's killers seemed to have got away with their foul deed.

Yet, if the law would not get the killers, then maybe belief would.

In bygone days many beliefs beyond science and law governed the lives of those who lived then. One such belief was that if the murderer were to touch the body of the victim, no matter how long the body had been dead, the crime would be revealed by the bleeding of the body.

Therefore, when Mrs Edden publicly bid Tylor to come touch Noble's body before it was buried and he refused, saying it was just an old wives' tale that stupid old women like her believed, others around town began to see the truth of her vision.

Others in Thame also thought it was Sewell and Tylor, as they had been seen that night as people had searched for Noble, washing their hands in the pond near the church. Suspicion only grew when Seymour the constable was threatened and told not to investigate the death any further. A few weeks later, Noble's son, who had taken over his father's business, was threatened one night when returning from market. In the darkness two figures came out of the gloom and caught up the reins on the horse pulling the cart, one man sneered:

'Boy! We are going to do the same to you as we did to your old man.'

'Yeah, do send him our regards when you see him,' snarled the other.

The lad recognised the voices as Sewell and Tylor who then tried to grab at the young man till he fought them off with his whip and hurried home.

The Eddens had to wait ten months to see any justice, when Sewell was arrested for another crime, and in his testimony he 'snitched' on Tylor as his accomplice. Tylor was arrested, but still without real evidence, and with Sewell's own mother calling her son an imbecile and urging the magistrates not to trust his testimony, Tylor was freed. Then the true horror that was Tylor came out, showing him to be of such a despicable nature as only the devil would care for him. On his way home, Tylor bought ribbons and danced a jig in front of the houses of all those people who testified against him to show them he was still free. The people of Thame feared that no one could stop the evil of these two men. Yet Sewell was about to be his friend's undoing.

After a few days Sewell was granted bail, but immediately was rearrested for stealing chickens, so he was immediately sentenced to fourteen years transportation. In order to get a lesser sentence, Sewell told the authorities that it had been them that had attacked Noble Eddens, but it had been Tylor who had smashed his head in with the stone breaker's hammer. This was all the evidence that was needed. Tylor was arrested and both were taken to Aylesbury.

They say that in the gaol at Aylesbury those who were to receive the death sentence would be visited by a ghostly flickering flame, known to the prisoners as the 'Wat'. This strange will-o'-the-wisp would show itself to the doomed prisoners so that before they even went to trial they would know their fate. I wonder if Tylor and Sewell glimpsed the Wat, for at their trial they were sentenced to be hanged on 8 March 1830 outside of Aylesbury Gaol.

A crowd of over 4,000 people, including Mrs Edden and her son, came to watch as the two men took their final moments. Yet, what might be imagined as a solemn occasion was on that day more of a penny dreadful performance. Sewell came out upon the platform waving at anyone he knew in the gathered crowd, and seemingly searching for someone in the crowd. Evidently, he found who he was looking for as he called out: 'Ah Mr Taylor, there you are! I am just going to die, and I hope I shall go to heaven. So Goodbye, Mr Taylor, Goodbye!'

Tylor was next to address the crowd, for all the world looking a miserable and nervous figure trembling as he spoke.

'My blessed brothers, I wish to say a few words to you before I quit this world, which will be in a few moments; and I hope you will all take warning by my untimely fate, though I am innocent of the act for which I am about to suffer. I am just going to leave this world and I solemnly declare that my life has been taken away by false swearers. I bear them no malice, but freely forgive them, and I hope God will bless you all.'

Tylor was overcome by it all and lost his speech for a moment, he was just about to regain it when the execution cap was pulled over his eyes and both villains were 'launched into eternity'. Afterwards their bodies were handed over to hospitals in London for dissection, to learn the inner mysteries of the body, and so maybe in the end some good did come from them.

Yet Noble's story is not over; he has been seen over the years standing at the side of the road waiting for those who are themselves heading for trouble. Maybe his bad fortune has turned into an omen of misfortune, or perhaps he is there to warn people of the danger coming their way.

3

# STORIES FROM
# MILTON KEYNES

## FROM-CRETE COWS AND ROUNDABOUTS

*What most people know about Milton Keynes is that it is new,
that it has concrete cows and a lot of roundabouts. So where
better to start a chapter about Milton Keynes.*

*What a lot of people don't realise is that Milton Keynes has
a connection to the ancient Greek myth of Theseus and the
Minotaur. The city of Knossos, which sits atop the labyrinth,
the home/prison of the Minotaur, was the first ever planned city
anywhere in the world. So, when the architects of Milton Keynes
needed a logo for the Milton Keynes Development Corporation,
they used the symbol that appears all over the ruins of the ancient
city of Knossos – the symbol of the Minoan axe. So, when people
talk about getting lost in the labyrinth of straight roads and
roundabouts in Milton Keynes, they had better take care not to
come face-to-face with the Minotaur.*

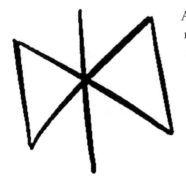

Although only fifty years old, the roundabouts of Milton Keynes are already steeped in legend – well, urban myth at least. Once upon a late night the planners of Milton Keynes were gathered round the latest design, arguing over what should go where or how big this should be or whether that road needed to be moved. Working late wasn't uncommon and so to keep the development warriors going, they brewed a magic potion, that late night cup of coffee.

As they poured over the plans, hour upon hour, changing this or changing that, coffee cups were placed hither and thither holding plans down, or simply being discarded as the next batch of hot dark elixir arrived. Finally, in the very early morning the designs were agreed and sent off.

The builders began their work and several weeks later the planners arrived to see how their designs were taking shape, but everywhere they looked they saw roundabouts. They weren't sure that they had put any in the plans so where had they come from? One of the planners asked the builder why they had built all the roundabouts. The builder replied: 'Well, they were all over the designs.'

'What?' cried the planners.

So the builder took out the plans and there, sure enough, all over the designs were light brown circles from where the coffee cups had sat.

# THE GUARDIAN

*Before there was the infamous new town of Milton Keynes, there was a small rural village with its quaint old houses, inn and church; an image that was a world away from a town renowned for its grid square road system. Yet this story heralds from those peaceful days before the new town came and took the name of this little village.*

There were once two brothers and their friend Billy Blunt who lived in Woughton-on-the-Green and, times being tough, they were always on the lookout for ways to make life easier for themselves. So, when one day one of the brothers noticed a lot of rabbit holes around the fields of Milton Keynes village, it seemed to him a good way of filling the cooking pot.

The fellow told his brother and Billy, and the three of them came up with a plan. To be caught poaching would mean big trouble with the law, so they decided it was best to go about their business when everyone else was in church for Sunday service. Everything was set: they had the dogs and the ferret, and next Sunday they would get them bunnies.

When Sunday came, the bells rang out calling folks to service, and by 10 a.m. the lanes were filled with people hurrying their way to church. The three poachers were already in the field at Milton Keynes, hiding behind the hedgerows, keeping the dogs quiet so no one would see them.

As the throng hurried by and the service began, the poachers set to work. They peeked out of their hiding place, first checking that the field was clear, and then the lanes. Not a person was in sight. The brother who had found the holes now knelt beside one with his ferret, ready to pop it down the hole and chase those rabbits out. His brother and Billy each held a dog that was eagerly awaiting the chase.

Just as the ferret was about to be placed down that hole, a sudden chill took the air and all three men looked up to see an incredibly tall strong fellow staring at them. He hadn't been there a moment ago, but there he stood, and he did not look happy.

Not saying a word, they just looked at each other, and carefully the ferret was placed back in its carry bag. The poachers, not wanting to fall foul of the law, started to back up, never letting their eyes drop from the stranger. Yet, as they scooped up their things, they momentarily looked down; when their eyes rose again, the stranger had gone.

A cold chill run over all of them. Was it a ghost? A guardian spirit of the wild things, or an angel sent to protect the innocent and remind the poachers where they should have been that Sunday? None of them knew, but they were 'frit

alf to deeth' and so away they ran back home, their Sunday pot-roast somewhat lacking, and they swore never to go a-poaching in Milton Keynes or on a Sunday ever again.

## HEART OF TREASON!

*The Gunpowder Plot was hatched right here in Milton Keynes. Near Newport Pagnell stands Gayhurst Manor, which in 1605 was owned by a man called Sir Everard Digby, known to be 'the finest gentleman in England'. Just from his name you can imagine the fine cut of the man, dressed in his doublet and hose. He was so well renowned that in 1603 he was knighted by James I, but he was also a Catholic when being a Catholic was a crime.*

Remember, remember the fifth of November,
Gunpowder treason and plot
I don't see no reason why gunpowder treason
Should ever be forgot.
A stick and a stake for King George's sake.
If you don't give me one I'll take two.
To rickety racket your door will go.
*(sung in North Bucks)*

People say that King Henry VIII did away with Catholicism because he wanted to divorce his wife, Catherine of Aragon. So, he broke off all ties with the Pope and formed the Anglican Church. But when his daughter Mary came to the throne, she brought Catholicism back and Protestants were persecuted. When she died and her sister Elizabeth wore the crown; the new Queen got rid of Catholicism again, so Catholics were now persecuted, and the Protestants were safe. So, when Elizabeth died and the crown passed to James I of England (James VI of Scotland) people wondered if there was going to be another change in the national religion. James knew he was in a tricky position and so he continued with the persecution of Catholics, which made him very unpopular. So, there were some Catholics who started to hatch a plan to kill the King and destroy his Parliament.

It is because of this religious persecution Sir Everard and people like him had to hide their faith, and at Gayhurst Manor they had a very clever way of doing it. He had a secret room built at Gayhurst and it was here that he came to know the Catholic Robert Catesby – the man who then introduced him to the legendary Guy Fawkes.

Fawkes needed somewhere to finalise his plans, somewhere close to London but far enough away so that he could do his plotting in private. When Guy Fawkes first came to Gayhurst, Sir Everard didn't want anything to do with the plot – he thought it too violent and that there had to be another way to do things. However, Guy Fawkes' silver tongue and the continuing persecution of the Catholics persuaded Sir Everard to change his mind and he paid £1,500 to support the plot – a huge amount of money in those days. Thus, Sir Everard was embroiled in the plot: the plans were made, the players were cast, and the action was set.

Guy Fawkes went to London in early November 1605, whilst Sir Everard travelled west to Worcestershire. The plan was for Sir Everard to appear to be on a hunting trip, when actually he was staying close to the manor house where Princess Elizabeth, James's daughter, was staying. In the aftermath of blowing up Parliament, Sir Everard was to take Princess Elizabeth hostage. Elizabeth would then be crowned the new Catholic queen and, once the plotters were in control of the crown, they would be able to end the persecution of the Catholics.

But an anonymous letter was sent to William Parker, the 4th Baron of Monteagle, revealing the plot and on 4 November Guy Fawkes was found in the vaults of Westminster with thirty-six barrels of gunpowder. The other plotters were soon rounded up, including Sir Everard Digby; they were tried for treason, found guilty and sentenced to be hung, drawn and quartered.

Sir Everard and the other plotters were taken through the streets of London to the place of execution. There they were hanged until they were unconscious and then taken down and placed on a table, where their guts were pulled out and placed on a brazier to burn whilst they were still alive. There is one other thing that the executioner does to a traitor, and that is to reach up through the traitor's chest and pull out their still beating heart and hold it up to the crowd and say: 'This be the heart of a traitor.'

But when they did this to Sir Everard, he cried out with his dying breath: 'Thou liest, Sir!'

## THE STONY GUNPOWDER PLOT

*On 25 November 1859 there was a gunpowder plot right here in Milton Keynes.*

There was once a gentleman whose name was George Atkins, who had opened a drapery business in New Bradwell, owned the Radcliffe Arms in Wolverton, and was running a grocery shop on the Stony Stratford High Street.

George, like all businessmen of his day, was a little on the Draconian side – it was the Victorian era after all. He may not have been as bad as Scrooge, but he did expect his workers to put in long days for little pay, which made him no different from many other businessmen. But George had a way of rubbing people up the wrong way. Therefore, he might not have been best loved by his workers.

It had been a long hard day in the grocery shop; with winter upon them, people were growing less in their own gardens and so the shop was busy. It was the end of the day and the shop assistant was sweeping the floor and preparing to close the shop and go home. By this time, George had gone into the back room to start counting the takings of the day and so the shop assistant was left alone to her work. The girl noticed a strange bit of rope leading to the stockroom. On closer inspection she saw that the rope was covered in saltpetre. This is not the type of salt to place on your chips, for it is highly explosive. She followed the rope to the stock-room door and, when she opened it, she saw that there was a trail of gunpowder leading to a large barrel of gunpowder in the stockroom.

Terrified out of her wits, the poor girl ran to alert George, who immediately called the authorities. When the police arrived and investigated the scene, they declared that there was enough gunpowder to not only blow up the shop but also the residence above, and it would certainly kill and injure many people.

The police asked George Atkins if he knew anybody who bore a grudge against him, and George had to admit that he could think of one or two people who he might have upset over the years, but that he would deal with it himself. So, the police dropped the case. As to how George dealt with the matter himself, we do not know but for the rest of his days there were no more gunpowder plots, so we can be sure that he dealt with it somehow.

## MISCHIEVOUS MONKS

*Tickford Priory was founded by Fulk Paganell in Newport Pagnell in 1140. It had sixteen French monks and was deemed 'alien' during the Hundred Years War, its income seized by the Kings Edward III and Richard the Lionheart.*

When Richard of Gravesend became the Bishop of Lincoln in the year of our Lord 1258 he set about reviewing all that came under his new diocese. As he read through the records, which contained the size, accounts, and number of brother/sisterhood for each monastery, he noticed Tickford Priory. Its land was considerable and produced a generous income from the many churches and tithes spread across a dozen parishes, yet in recent years it seemed that the numbers of new novices had dwindled and reports suggested a very lax approach to the usual routines of prayer, fasting, and grounds work. The bishop set out to investigate and when he found the reports were true he chastised the prior and told him to turn the situation around.

By 1275, Tickford Priory had become quite the headache of Bishop Richard, and he found that things had not improved; if anything, they had become worse. So, it was decided that the best course of action was to appoint a new prior. Please welcome to the scene Simon de Reda.

If Bishop Richard had hoped that Prior Simon would turn around the situation at Tickford Priory then he was about to be very sorely upset. Simon was not as you might expect a typical prior to be, and if the priory had been bad before, it was about to get a whole lot worse.

Simon enjoyed the finer things of life and didn't see why he should be denied his earthly pleasures. As prior, he led his brotherhood into a never-ending party of 'drinking, cavorting, and wasting goods of the monastery'. Food wasn't being shared amongst the poor, but instead was being consumed at revelries that lasted days, and even involved alcohol, women and, well, whatever else was on offer. Even the monastery money was used for more fashionable clothing than the usual monk's habit and to buy all manner of trinkets. The priory looked less like a house of the holy and more like a house of ill repute as the brothers became ever more outrageous in their festivities.

The position of Bishop of Lincoln had now passed to Oliver Sutton, and if Tickford Priory had been a headache to his predecessor, it was now the devil's own headache for Bishop Oliver.

First, Bishop Oliver had Simon excommunicated for his unholy leadership of the Tickford brethren, but this did little good because the monks quite liked their new life and didn't want to let Simon de Reda go. Simon pleaded that he was the injured party and had been imprisoned by the riotous monks, so he was reinstated and continued in the role of prior. However, the trouble at Tickford continued despite numerous warnings.

This was outrageous behaviour, and an incredible insult to Bishop Oliver and the Church. So, the good bishop had the Undersheriff of Buckinghamshire, Reginald de Grey, seize the priory and all of its land, and cast out the badly behaving monks and their ringleader.

Unbelievably, Simon still managed to hold onto his position as prior, and it wasn't long before the unruly monks were back and up to their old tricks.

By 1290, Bishop Oliver resolved to deal with the problem once and for all, so he planned a personal visit to deal with Simon face to face. When he arrived, the monks were waiting outside the priory for him, for they had heard that Bishop Oliver was coming, but this was no welcoming party. Like a renegade army they gathered, clutching candlesticks, garden tools, and whatever else they could find, to bar the bishop from entering the priory. Try as he might, Bishop Oliver just could not gain access, and all the while Simon was safely inside the priory, drinking to his bishop's health.

Reports continued to come in every day with complaints from the people of Newport Pagnell, who had to deal with these unruly religious rioters. More complaints were made of 'wasting goods, evil living' and even murder, until finally there was enough to bring charges against Simon and depose him as prior. In 1291 Simon was gone, and the Bishop of Lincoln breathed a sigh of relief.

Yet bad 'habits' are hard to lose. In 1340, the Bishop of Lincoln was (another bad boy of the Church) Henry Burgwash (see Greenman of Fingest). Bishop Henry received accounts that all out warfare had arisen between the monks of Tickford and the local vicar and parishioners. The current prior, Fulk de Champaigne, and a few of the other monks had besieged the vicarage and set about breaking down doors, smashing windows, and yelling insults at the vicar. When the poor man tried to sneak out of a window to escape, Prior Fulk and his followers caught him, beat and wounded him, and then stole £10 worth of goods from him.

Finally, the Tickford Priory was closed by Cardinal Wolsey in 1524 to pay towards Christchurch in Oxford, and this silenced the turbulent Tickford Priory forever.

## THE DEVIL'S HOUSE

*Olney, in the northern tip of Buckinghamshire, is famous for two things. Firstly, as the home of poet William Cowper and Rector John Newton (who wrote the hymn 'Amazing Grace'); together they wrote a number of hymns, still sung today. Secondly, it holds an annual pancake race on Shrove Tuesday that is open to all residents of Olney.*

*They say the tradition began in the 1400s when a housewife was hurriedly using up the last of the dairy foods before Lent. With her headscarf and apron on, she made her batter and took up her frying pan until it was hot on the fire. As she poured the last of the mixture into the pan, the shriving bells rang out from the church calling everyone for service. With frying pan still in hand, tossing the pancake as she went, the woman ran to the church and left her pan by the font while she attended service. However, we are concerned here with the darker side of Olney … a more devilish side.*

It was midnight and a carriage was charging down the Warrington Road at full pelt. The four horses pulling the coach were as black darkness, and were remarkable for their speed, strength, and lack of heads. The coachmen too were headless, for sat inside this careering carriage was the devil himself and he had business in Olney.

As the road neared the pond, the carriage broke from the road and ran straight into the water with such force that it was called Whirly Pond ever after. From here, the dark lord's coach travelled underground, causing the earth to shake for miles around. Near Goosey Bridge the carriage burst forth from the underworld so violently that the earth erupted in a great funnel straight up into the air, and the whole meadow swayed and shuddered for so many years after that it was called Sway Gog.

Finally, the carriage came to rest in the high street just besides a large house (now split into No. 121, 123A and 125A). This was the home of Dr John Faust, who had long ago made a deal with the devil and had been tormented ever since. The doctor had fallen into a deep melancholy for now the time approached for the devil to collect his side of the bargain and end Dr Faust's life. The devil rapped on the door four times and without any assistance the door opened of its own accord and in strolled Old Scratch. Dr Faust fell to his knees and pleaded, begged, and prayed, but it was too late, a deal was a deal, and if he wouldn't come willingly then he would come anyway. With a jerk of his hand the devil invisibly caused the doctor to rise in the air so fast that his brains were dashed out on the ceiling.

That is how the devil moved into Olney, and took Dr Faust's soul but kept his spirit as company, and they say Dr Faust's ghost still resides there to this day.

Having the devil come to town caused quite the commotion and gossip throughout the town. Just opposite the devil's house lived a God-fearing old woman who always knew every bit of gossip concerning everyone in town. The old woman knew that from her topmost window in her attic she could look straight into the rooms of the devil's house, so she took to leaning out of her window and spying upon his every move.

This drove the devil mad; he closed the curtains, he pulled faces at her, he showed and shook his hairy red-tailed bottom at her, but still she pryed. How was he supposed to get on with any truly devilish plans if this woman gawped at him all the while? He pulled at his beard, and then at his tail, and finally at his horns in despair. Then a wonderfully wicked idea came to him.

As she stood, straining out of the window like a curtain in the wind, the devil glared at her with a wry smile and, with a click of his fingers, a set of enormous horns were suddenly placed atop her head. So heavy were they she could hardly lift her head, so large were they that she couldn't withdraw her head from the window.

The devil was so amused by his handiwork that he jigged and laughed all about the high street, his cloven feet tapping a merry beat as the woman above wailed and screamed for help. Her neighbours dashed to her assistance, but no matter how hard they pulled, the old woman remained stuck fast.

By sundown the woman was still there howling and wailing, bawling and weeping until the devil felt all this noise was far more annoying than the spying had ever been. And so, with a click of his fingers, the horns vanished and at last the woman was free, but she had learnt her lesson and never spied or gossiped ever again.

Done with this mischief, the devil decided to visit the local taproom, the Two Brewers. When he swept in through the door, a hush came over the room. The locals froze mid conversation and looked down into their tankards and pots so as not to make eye contact. The devil strode over to the landlord and derided him on having the quietest, most boring tavern in the world, and that it was the landlord's job to cheer it up. With one clap of the devil's hands, the landlord suddenly found himself jigging about the room, dancing and whirling and singing. He tried to stop by clinging to table, chair or person, but the devil simply shook his head: 'Uh-uh-uh! Where is the fun in that,' and so the landlord carried on, simply sweeping up anything or anyone he grabbed as a makeshift dance partner.

The locals looked on in horror, and when the devil noticed he declared: 'Well? Laugh then!' and so against their own will, the tavern's clientele found themselves laughing. The devil drank his fill, and only when he left did the peace return to the Two Brewers. When the devil returned the following night, and the next and so on, to do more of the same, soon people avoided going there, until the landlord was short of coin.

In desperation the landlord begged for help from the church. The next time the devil came in he saw, sat around a table, thirteen hooded figures, and he was just getting ready for some fun, when with terrible realisation the devil saw that they were thirteen priests with bell, Bible and candle. The candles were lit, the bells rang out, and when one began to read from the Bible, the devil found he couldn't run for the door.

One priest cried out: 'Leave this man and this town alone and never come back for 100 years.'

'And why should I do that when I am having such fun here? What do you know about fun? You are one of those boring priests, all bells and no balls. How dull! Not like those monks over at Tickford Priory, now they knew how to party!'

'Well then, will you leave this place until this candle I hold in my hand burns out?' asked a priest a little wiser than the rest.

'Huh! Of course. Gives me an hour or two to change my outfit.' And with that the devil vanished.

The priest quickly blew out the candle so it would not burn and threw it into the deepest well he could. So, thus, the candle has never burnt out and the devil had to leave Olney, for a deal is a deal!

For a while, the devil's house stood empty, no one daring to move in, until a stout-hearted man bought it, not minding at all the blood stain on the ceiling. On his first night in the house he unpacked a few things and wearily prepared himself for bed.

Closing his curtains, he got into bed and laid down ready for sleep. Yet shining full into his face was the bright moon. When the man looked, he saw his curtains were fully open. Sure that he had closed them, he got up and closed them again, and returned to bed, only to find they were open once more. Getting up once more, he looked around the room and saw sitting in the chair on the other side of the window the devil himself, who placed a finger to his lips and 'shhh'ed with a devilish smile.

Not to be outdone, the man pulled up a second chair beside the window on the opposite side of the room and shut the curtains. So, the devil got up and opened them and the man closed them and then the devil opened them. This went on until both competitors were exhausted and the sunlight broke the night's darkness. Losing all the fun out of this game, and seeing the fellow was as strong willed as he, the devil truly left Olney and so this story ends.

# A COCK AND BULL STORY

*If you go to the market town of Stony Stratford, people there will proudly tell you that the phrase a 'Cock and Bull' story originated in that town, for proudly sitting on the high street, and not fifty yards from each other, is the Bull Hotel and the Cock Hotel. Both these establishments, along with many other taverns and inns in Stony Stratford, were used at the height of the stagecoach days. Stony Stratford is exactly halfway between London and Birmingham on the old Roman road, the Watling Street, and it was said that travellers travelling between the two great cities would meet in Stony Stratford and share stories. These stories would get wilder and wilder as each traveller try to outdo the next, creating cock and bull stories. However, this is a Cock and Bull story in itself because the phrase 'Cock and Bull' story was being used in literature before these two inns were established. But let's not let truth get in the way of a good story, so here is one of the local origin myths of the phrase.*

There was once a man travelling from Birmingham to London by stagecoach. The ride was bumpy and hard for the roads were little more than dirt tracks. He soon became tired and sore, and longed to reach Stony Stratford where they would stop for the night. As they left Northampton, two more gentlemen joined him in the carriage who were also destined for Stony Stratford for they worked in the rival inns. One gentleman worked for the Cock Hotel and the other gentlemen worked for the Bull Hotel, and as soon as they heard that the first gentleman would be spending the night in Stony Stratford, both men expressed the virtues of their place of employment.

'You want to come and stay at the Cock Hotel – we serve the finest ale.'

'No, no! You must come and stay at the Bull Hotel – we serve the best meals.'

'Well, the beds at the Cock Hotel are softer.'

'Well, the rooms at the Bull Hotel are quieter.'

'That is because nobody in their right mind would stay there.'

And so on and so forth did the two gentlemen bicker, fighting over the traveller as the carriage rattled its way southward until it was just outside Stony Stratford. The poor traveller had put up with this arguing for nearly an hour and now his wits were frayed, his bones were sore, and his temper was erupting.

He pulled a pistol out from his belt and fired a bullet through the roof of the carriage. The carriage driver stopped the coach to see what the matter was, and the moment the vehicle stopped the traveller leapt from the carriage and ran off into the night screaming, 'Enough of these Cock and Bull stories!'

## BREAD, BEER AND BEEF!

*When what locals tend to think of as Wolverton was first estab-lished to house the many railway workers of the Wolverton Works, it was called Wolverton Station, for it grew up around about what is now quite a modest railway station. There had been a medieval village called Old Wolverton that had been abandoned and a watermill called Wolverton Mill so it was not surprising for the name to be adopted. It was 17 September 1838 that the actual train station opened.*

Down at Euston Station, there was quite the event happen-ing. People had crammed in to get a look at the gleaming train that would be the first to carry passengers north to Wolverton Station. Those first passengers were all sorts of dignitaries, dressed in their finest clothes. There was George Carr Glynn, the chairman of the works. There was Edward Bury, the locomotive superintendent who designed the engine, and Richard Creed, the secretary of Wolverton Works. There was the engineer Robert Stephenson. There was also the Duke of Sussex. They all boarded, and the steam locomotive started to make its way up the line.

It took two hours for the steam locomotive to huff and puff its way through field and village until it finally reached Wolverton Station. When that great iron engine with its grinding wheels finally entered the station and stopped, a great puff of steam erupted from its funnel, which seemed to signal the start of the celebration and everybody cheered. It was like a county fair. There were stalls and booths every-where selling food and entertainment. There was fun to be had by all, and most of the Wolverton Works employees had even been given the day off to enjoy it. And to top it all, they were given free bread, beer, and beef! It was an exceptional day. They say the celebration started at the station and went all the way into Stony Stratford, some two miles down the Wolverton Road.

The dignitaries left the train to make all of their speeches and meet the workers. Then they had to wait about for an hour because that's how long it took to get a new engine put on the train to take it further up the track. Finally, dignitaries got back on board, the people cheered them off and away went the train.

About an hour later, the next train came through, this one filled with first-class carriages and gentlemen's carriages. Just like the previous locomotive, this too was welcomed with great excitement and a huge cheer. More free bread, beer and beef were given out and whilst the passengers waited for the engine to be swapped over, some visited the stalls and booths whilst others admired the new town then being built for the railway workers. Finally, the passengers boarded and that train also departed.

About an hour later, the people at Wolverton Station expected the next train, but they waited, and they waited, and they waited. But no train arrived. It was the first of many a delayed train. Suddenly, news came through that just outside of Wolverton the fire basket had dropped off the train and it could go no further. Eager to get more free bread beer and beef, the workers grabbed their tools and dashed down the track to fix the problem.

Finally, three hours late, the train chugged into Wolverton station with some very weary workers and passengers. But the crowd that was still waiting gave the train such a cheer that it lifted the spirits of workers and passengers alike. The train driver was most bemused and asked why everybody was cheering when they were so late. And they told him that once his train left, which was the last train of the day, then the celebrations would be over, and so his delayed train had extended that great day by an extra three hours. And so, they had enjoyed more free bread, beer and beef. So, it would seem that the very first delayed train was not a great cause of misery.

## THE GRAVE ROBBERS

*This story focuses on the Magdalene Tower in Stony Stratford. It used to be part of the Mary Magdalene Church until the great fire of Stony Stratford in 1742 burned down the main part of the church, leaving just the tower. Browne Willis, a famous antiquarian from Fenny Stratford, paid to secure the roof and shore up the tower and he bid the people of Stony Stratford to repair the church. However, Stony Stratford had two churches that had divided the parish, the other being St Giles, which had also been damaged in the fire, and so they chose to unite the parish by repairing just the one church, and the church they chose to save was St Giles. St Magdalene's, therefore, was never rebuilt, and the tower was left standing. The graveyard remained in use until 1870. The tower, however, fell into disrepair until National Lottery funding in 2015 was used to repair it and tidy the graveyard.*

It was a Monday in November when the rain drummed down on Stony Stratford and the cobblers were enjoying their day off and spending their weekly wages in the Windmill Inn. They'd been there for a few hours, passing round the pewter pots of ales, playing skittles, then cards, and swapping stories when they noticed the six o'clock coach from Birmingham go past.

A short while later, two bearded men with faces that showed a life of hard work walked in. They seemed to be navvies by the pickaxe and spade they had slung on their backs, maybe come to work on the railroad that was being built over Wolverton. They had thick Irish accents and asked the landlord if there was a room for the night, which the landlord swiftly arranged for them. The pair secluded themselves in the corner of the pub furthest from the cobblers, keeping themselves to themselves whilst they ate a modest supper of bread and cheese, but soon got to arguing about the location of the old churchyard. By the way they talked about the streets, it was obvious they had been to Stony Stratford before.

As the evening settled in, the landlord lit the 'rushlight dips made in the old candle chandlery in the Whitehorse yard'. The cobblers continued with their games and after about an hour noticed the two Irish lads getting themselves ready to go up to their room. The cobblers heard the navvies' heavy boots on the stairs to the rooms above and all went quiet.

By now, the cobblers had been drinking for a few of hours. They played dominoes until they 'couldn't tell the blank from the double six' and took to singing. Welsh Johns the tailor climbed upon the table and sung his heart out until he tumbled down. Billy Richardson called for quiet as above they heard those heavy boots on the stairs. Fearing they had woken the navvies and were about to be for it, the cobblers and tailor fell out of the pub bidding goodnight to the landlord.

As they passed the Old Magdalene churchyard, still in high spirits, Billy turned to his friends: 'Boys, my boys! I'll wager a new hat or a pound to the man who is game enough to venture in to the churchyard and bring back a sprig of alder.' Billy stayed with Johns who was still recovering from his tumble, but the other two lands were game for the dare with a chance of winning a new hat or a pound. At the time, there were two alder trees growing in the church yard: one by the furthest wall of the graveyard, and the other one growing from the top of the tower, which was in such a sorry state of repair those days.

The daring two set their sights on the alder tree by the wall, but it was hard to set their sights on anything as a fog came on. As they crept around the tower, they suddenly noticed a light moving in the mist. Their hearts stopped as they watched the ghostly light bob about, and the terrible sound of pounding as though something was trying its utmost to break free from the holy soil.

But as they watched, they realised that the truth was even worse than their imagined nightmare, for there in the graveyard were the two Irish lads digging up a grave. The darers could just make out the navvies, one holding the lamp and the other sorting through a pile of bones and plundering trinkets and jewellery into a small bag. They were grave robbers!

The navvies, hearing the sudden movement near the tower, abandoned their grisly work and leapt over the wall and were off. The next day the local constable, Ashton, found the shovels, but after an investigation couldn't find the villains, but then some did say he couldn't catch a cold in his vest. The cobblers kept quiet for fear of being accused of being accomplices and exported or, even worse, ending up on the medical table themselves.

## THE WITCH OF HORSEFAIR GREEN

*Horsefair Green is a long rectangle of grass lined by lime trees, which today makes a very pleasant place for a picnic. At one end is the Stony Stratford war memorial and at the other end a path that leads to the high street. But many years ago, this was where horses were brought every Friday to be bought and sold, hence its name Horsefair Green. Over the years it has also been a saw pit, and then illegal extensions to people's gardens, and now each year it holds the 'Folk on the Green' festival in early June. But a long time ago it was the home of a witch.*

Once there was a witch who lived on Horsefair Green, in the thatched cottage with the sundial over the porch. She was as ugly as a witch ought to be in a story, with her face lined and showing nearly a century-old life. She walked with a stoop and an old ash walking stick, a crimson shawl and a wide-brimmed bonnet.

Some said she had learnt her healing powers from the monks who used to live many years ago at the 'retreat'. Others said she had made a deal with Old Scratch, and there were those who thought that her magical skills came from nature itself through the spirits of the trees and the plants.

But, wherever her skills came from, there was no doubting she was good at what she did. People from all around would walk miles to come and receive the cures for broken hearts or smallpox, sore eyes, even the king's evil; she could cure them all. Her main ingredient came from a local sacred well in Calverton called Gorrick's Spring, and she would make her way there every day, come rain or shine, snow or thunder, to fetch a bucket of that sacred water. And as she stooped over the world to collect the precious liquid, she would say these words:

> When Gorrick's Spring runs fast and clear
> Stoop down and drink for health is here
> If Gorrick's Spring should e'er run dry
> Beware for the pestilence is nigh.

But as the years rolled by, the old crone found that her bones creaked, and her muscles ached under the effort of carrying all those buckets of water every day from Calvert back to Horsefair Green. And so, she got herself an apprentice; a mysterious young girl whom the old witch adopted. They say the girl was as charming and beautiful as the old crone was ugly: she had hair as black as a raven's wing, eyes as blue as a cloudless sky, lips as ruby red as the holly berries, framing a glittering pearl white smile.

The girl was a good lass and each and every single day she went down to Calverton and collected the water, saying the rhyme just like the old witch had taught her. During the day she would help tidy the old woman's cottage and listen as people came with their worries and woes, ailments and urgencies. The girl watched and she learned that sometimes a conversation and a cup of tea with a sprig of sage were all that some needed, whilst others needed strange and elaborate potions to be created from herbs that grew on the banks of the River Ouse. Each day, the girl learnt some new wise cunning to aid the poor and the sick, the hopeless and the downhearted. And as time went by, the girl grew to a beautiful young woman who, rather than watching, helped the old witch in all matters.

Yet the girl herself still did not have the gift of healing, no matter how hard she tried; as she mixed the potions, or brewed the tea, it just didn't seem to have the same effect as a cure that the old witch made. All will come with time, croaked the old witch; don't be in such a hurry to wish your life away. When the time is right your power will come. And so, the girl continued learning, mixing, brewing, and fetching the water each day.

It was on one such bright June day, when the sun was shining and the sky was clear, that the girl took a moment down by Gorrick's Spring to feel the heat on her face. The lark began to sing, then the thrush joined in, and the blackbird in the woods called its song, the wind blew through the grass and insects droned until it felt that all of nature were singing a song just for her.

Suddenly, the birds became quiet and the girl became aware of another sound of snuffling and footsteps coming towards her. There she saw a scruffy little dog urging its way towards her with its master being pulled along behind. The dog leapt up at the girl and began to lick her face. Its master called the dog to heel and apologised to the girl. It was then, the girl realised, that the lad before her – handsome and tanned – was a blind gypsy pedlar, a lad just a bit older than herself.

'Good Morning sir. You and your dog look thirsty travelling this hot dusty road.'

'Good morning to you. Can you guide me to the water's edge?'

The girl offered the lad her pitcher so he didn't need to stoop and settled him down on the edge of the spring. As she scooped out the water, she spoke the rhyme, for she was so used to doing it when collecting water from the spring. The lad drank deeply.

'Who taught you those fines words?' asked the lad.

'My grandmother. I come by this way every day and say the words so to fetch the healing waters.'

'If she has the power to heal, I would most dearly like to meet her, for maybe she could help my eyes.'

As suddenly as if she had known what to do her whole life, the girl took from her pocket a red handkerchief and spoke a new rhyme:

> Stoop, gypsy stoop for health is here,
> Bathe those sightless eyes in waters clear
> Maybe you shall see anew
> Return the sight to eyes so blue

The lad held out his hand to be guided to the water's edge, she handed him her red kerchief, which he dipped into the water. As the water soaked into the red kerchief the dyes started to leach out and spread across the surface of the water as red as blood. Now as pale as snow, the lad washed his eyes with that kerchief, then gasped as he blinked; suddenly he could see!

For the very first time he could see the spring, he could see the blue sky, he could see his scruffy dog, and he could see the girl, and he could even see that, without compare, she was beautiful. In that moment he was enraptured.

'Surely you are a gift from heaven, an angel? I shall love thee all my days and be thy slave for all my days.'

'I need no thanks, or everlasting debt. I live to heal, to help and to care for all things. However, I would appreciate one kindness – could you carry my pitcher of water?'

When the girl realised that she had cured the boy's blindness she wished to hurry back to Horsefair Green to tell her grandmother what had happened. For as much joy as she felt over curing the lad, she couldn't help feeling something was wrong with her grandmother and hurried back home.

The girl called to the old crone when she arrived, but there was no answer. In the kitchen there sat the ancient woman still and unmoving in her old chair. She did not stir, nor did she wake, for in the moment that the girl had cured the gypsy lad's blindness the crone had passed from this life to the next, and so her power had passed to the girl. She was buried in the old churchyard by the tower where there grew an alder tree.

The gypsy lad stayed with the girl, devoted and true, fetching the water from Gorrick's Spring each day. Eventually they married, and their cures and potions were passed on to their children ever after.

## POLLY PARROT

*This is a story, or rather a personal tale, told by Hawtin Mundy to the Living Archive in Milton Keynes. Hawtin was born and bred in New Bradwell and, before he died, he recorded many tapes telling the story of his life and giving shape to the past of the local area. Since the development of Milton Keynes, the Living Archive has collected the oral histories of residents, both original inhabitants and the migrating settlers who began to arrive in the early 1970s. This archive is an extraordinary account of the people who have shaped the largest and most successful new town in Britain.*

When Hawtin Mundy was a lad in New Bradwell, he and his best friend Ginger used to run out of school at the end of the day and head straight for the baker's shop. It wasn't that they were particularly hungry, nor was it that the baker had created any irresistible cakes. Oh no, the reason the boys ran to the bakery was that old Scotty Edwards the baker had a pet parrot that could talk. The boys would delight in getting Polly to chat, and over the years the parrot had even learnt the names of some of the boys. So that every time Hawtin and Ginger went into the shop the parrot would call out Ginger's name loud and shrill. 'GINGER!!!! GINGER!!!!'

Time ticked on, and old Scotty Edwards decided that it was time to retire, so he sold up the shop and got himself a brand new house built just down by the newly constructed canal. It was a lovely house and it suited Scotty and Polly just fine. Down at the bottom of the garden there was a lovely old tree that overhung the walkway by the canal, and each morning Scotty would go and hang Polly's cage up in the tree so she could watch as the canal boats pulled by ponies drifted by. In those days, ponies pulled the canal boats because they didn't have engines, and the canal boat drivers, known as boaties, would call commands to their ponies: 'Gee up!' to get the ponies to walk on, and 'Whoa!' to make them stop.

Polly heard the boatmen calls of 'Whoa' and 'Gee up' each day and soon she learnt to give the same calls. A pony would be trotting along when suddenly Polly would call out 'Whoa!'

and the pony would come to a sudden halt. The boatie would call to his pony to move on but the parrot would tell it to stop, and, just as the boatie got off the boat to move his pony along, Polly would call 'Gee up!' and off the pony would trot, leaving the boatie to run behind. As you can imagine, the boaties weren't best pleased and they made all sorts of threats to ring that parrot's neck, but no one ever did.

However, one cold autumn evening Scotty forgot to bring Polly in. I've heard rumour tell that it was because the boaties took old Scotty Edwards out for a drink and made sure he was good and inebriated before they took him home. So, when he awoke the next day, he saw that there had been a hard frost on the ground and realising that he left Polly out there all night he ran down to the bottom of the garden, but it was too late – poor old Polly had frozen to death.

And, were we to leave it here, this would indeed be a sad old tale, but what Hawtin remembers shows us that in every life, and in every place, a little bit of magic can exist. For Hawtin tells us that, since that day, ponies trotting along by the canal, stop when they reach the tree that Polly used to sit in, and they bow their heads as if in atonement for what their masters had done. And nobody says 'Whoa!'

## DICK TURPIN

*Dick Turpin legends appear across the country, and, despite being so new, Milton Keynes is no different.*

Dick Turpin used to frequent the routes around Woughton-on-the-Green and the Watling Street. It was said that he used the ancient trackways such as Bury Lane, which lead off into the Watling Street. At the junction of the ancient trackway and the Roman road sat the Old Swan, and the landlord there was a friend of Dick Turpin's, for it always 'paid' to help a highwayman.

Dick would watch the passing trade from the window upstairs, known jokingly as the 'prison room'. Once he picked his quarry he would then set off. One day he was planning a daring hold-up and, before he set off, he went to the local blacksmith and paid him handsomely to re-shoe Black Bess. This was nothing unusual. But when Dick told the blacksmith to put the shoes on in the reverse direction, the blacksmith thought him quite mad, but thought wiser than to utter his musing out loud. The blacksmith's skilled hands worked swiftly and productively. The great furnaces were stoked, and with his thick leather apron on, and hammer in hand, the smithy got to work. In no time at all the blacksmith had taken the shoes from Black Bess's hooves, turned them around and replaced each shoe.

So, when Dick Turpin rode off to Traps Hill in Loughton to make his hold-up, it looked like he was riding in the opposite direction! This quite confused the authorities and allowed Dick to escape and call out, 'Stand and deliver' another day.

And on the 'another day', Dick was again riding down the Watling with the authorities close behind him. He needed somewhere to hide so he rode fast into Stony Stratford because there he had yet another friend who was a landlord.

Some tellers of this tale will say it was the White Horse pub; others say it was the Talbot Inn, but in either case it was on the Calverton parish side of the high street because the buildings on that side have no basements, as the Ouse used to flood regularly. So, the beer could not be kept in cellars, instead it was winched up and kept in the attics.

When Dick told his landlord friend he needed somewhere to hide, his friend at first said no – if the authorities saw Black Bess (who was nearly as famous as Dick Turpin himself) in the stables they would know Dick was hiding there. Just then, the bar ran out of ale, and the skinny lad who was the bar hand began to grumble about having to winch down another barrel.

The landlord and Dick looked at each other and smiled. Moments later, Black Bess was harnessed to the winch and, pulling with all their might, Dick, the landlord and the bar hand swiftly but carefully lifted the whinnying horse into the air higher and higher until she was at the attic hatch.

There in the attic, Dick and Bess hid for three days, until the authorities were well and truly gone. Then they winched Bess back down, and Dick rode off out of this story and into many others.

## Tally Ho! Hanmer

*The Hanmer Family have been important and influential in Simpson ever since 1717 when Susan Walden, heiress of the manor of Simpson, married Job Hanmer. In the Simpson parish records there are two Hanmers: Graham Hanmer (n.d.) and Thomas Walden Hanmer (1807) who served as rector, but as the story contains no dates or first names it is difficult to know which Hanmer is Tally Ho!*

The Hanmer family have been important in the history of Simpson since the 1700s, and they were a wealthy family who, as landowners of the area, set up charitable funds for the area. So, it is no great surprise to find that two members of the family have served as rectors in the local church of St Thomas the Apostle. It appears that in every family there is a lovable rogue.

He was known to one or more as 'Tally Ho! Hamner', for the rector of Simpson loved to dress in hunting attire with 'mahogany coloured top boots and a square cut riding coat, black breeches and a low black hat with a broad flat brim'. Tally Ho had earned himself the reputation of being a reckless foxhunting debtor of a parson and yet his parishioners loved him for his lively services and generosity to the community. Should debt collectors turn up to the rectory house, they would find their way barred by obstacles and locals alike.

He was very good at tapping people for money with such sob stories that would make your heart bleed, and in this fashion, borrowing from old college friends.

On one occasion, he was down in London enjoying a bit of the high life, when he bumped into an old friend and they got to chatting and sharing a drink or two. But when it came time for the bill, Hamner found he was 'a little short'.

'That is not the worst of it, dear chap. I must get home to my parish in Simpson to perform Sunday duties and it would appear I have no money for travel. Whatever am I to do?' bewailed the rector.

Dutifully, being of a good nature, and never one to deprive a congregation of their rector, the friend offered Tally Ho £5 to get him home. The relieved parson thanked his friend a thousand times over for his good nature and blessed him for being such a good soul. With that, they parted ways.

Later that day, the good Samaritan bumped into an old friend and told him of his earlier good deed helping Tally Ho get back to Simpson. The friend congratulated him on being so charitable and in celebration of such a deed offered him dinner at the Long Hotel in Bond Street, and off they went with eager hunger.

But, as they passed through the doors, who should they see tucking into a fine dinner and champagne but the beleaguered rector, who rather than becoming bashful at having been caught out instead brazened out the situation and even went on to a play after his meal.

The good Samaritan was aghast at such behaviour from a rector, but this lovable rogue was still adored by his parishioners despite his failings.

## PENNY A PEEK

*In Stony Stratford's Market Square there is now only one pub, the Crown (which famously featured in the film* Withnail and I*) but in years past there were many more taverns surrounding the square, one of which was the King's Head, the name of which can still be seen on the front door of the building.*

Many years ago, the feisty landlady of the King's Head in Stony Stratford had a son called Constable. Try as she might, she could not get that boy to behave; he was always up to some trick or trouble. They say he could even lie straight in bed.

Well, Constable fell in with a bad lot and he took to stealing sheep, which in those days was punishable by hanging. Unfortunately for Constable, it turned out he wasn't a very good sheep stealer and he was soon caught. He was charged at the assizes at the county hall in Aylesbury and sentenced to be hanged. On the day of his execution he was taken to 'the drop' – the hanging scaffold installed on the main balcony of the county hall. There he was hung by his neck until he was dead.

His mother came forward to collect the body and return it to Stony Stratford for burial. However, just before the burial was planned,

Stony Stratford had one of its many fairs that it is famous for and, so that her time had not been a complete loss, Constable's mother came up with a plan to recoup some of the money and effort she'd put into bringing up that ne'er-do-well. In one of the top rooms at the King's Head, she put her dead son on display and charged a penny a peek to come and see the hanged man.

## THE TALLEST SPIRE IN BUCKS

*Hanslope Church's spire once measured 200 feet tall (61m) which was its height during this next story. In 1804 the spire was hit by lightning and had to be rebuilt, yet at 186ft it is still the tallest spire in Buckinghamshire.*

*'If Hanslope spire were ten times higher I'd take off my shoe and jump it over!' (A local saying)*

The church in the little village of Hanslope had the tallest spire in all of Buckinghamshire, so you can imagine when the weathervane broke and risked further damage to the spire, it was indeed a tall problem. The people of Hanslope put an advert in the paper to help save their tall spire. For such a problem, there could only be one man to fix it and his name was Robert Cadman. Robert was a steeplejack famed for never using scaffolding, instead he would climb nimbly like a mountaineer to the very tip of the spire, and he did so with a drum strapped to his back on which he would play a tattoo when he reached the top so that all could hear.

He answered the advert and was quickly sent for. When he arrived in Hanslope, there was a lot of excitement and people came out to see as he made his way down the street and to the church. They gathered round and they watched in awe and expectation as he sprightly clambered up the stone spire and up to the very top. Once there he gathered his drum and beat such a tattoo of celebration that the people beneath cheered, and then Robert set to work.

As it turned out there was quite a lot of damage to the old spire, and so Robert worked hard racing the daylight to finish his job and, as the light began to dwindle, the job was completed with barely enough light for his descent to the ground. Quickly he gathered up his tools and as the crowd watched (there's always a crowd for a dangerous task) he started to make his way back down. As he reached the ground another great cheer went up, everyone wanted to shake his hand or slap his back, and many good ales were offered in the public house where Robert and the crowd soon retired.

The people of Hanslope were delighted that the famous Robert Cadman had fixed their spire, and Robert found that, although he never paid for a drink all night, he was never short of a pint in his hand. After a couple of hours, praise gave way to stories and singing, and Robert reached for his drum to play a beat along with the tune that danced all around. But when he sought his drum, he realised that he must have left it on the top of the spire.

Cadman was all for heading back to the steeple to retrieve his drum because being left out over-night would not do it any good all. But now it was dark with hardly enough moonlight to stagger home, and he had been drinking. Much

to Robert's reluctance, the good people of Hanslope finally convinced him not to climb, and to fetch his drum instead in the morning, but the joy of the evening had waned somewhat, and Robert was soon away to his bed.

At the first light of dawn Robert was awake and, feeling slightly sore headed, he set off for the church. Once again, he treated the people of Hanslope to the spectacle of his daring climb to reach the top of the spire and reclaim his drum, which was hanging on the weathervane. He played a short tattoo for the small gathered crowd before he climbed back down and, bidding farewell to the people of Hanslope, he continued his way to clamber up many more churches and buildings.

## MADAME BENNETT

*Galley Hill was one of the first housing estates built as part of the Milton Keynes new town development. Therefore, many of its residents who had migrated from outside of the local area believe that it has no history or heritage. But as this story shows, something has happened everywhere, even in places we think are inherently new.*

Simon Bennett had been a Roundhead in the Civil War but, being a good man, had received a full pardon when King Charles II was restored. He and his wife Grace lived at Calverton Manor farm, and Simon was as good-natured and kindly as the year was long. He gave to the poor in Stony Stratford and Calverton, making sure they had bread and ale. He let them gather fallen wood on his land, as was the tradition at the time, so that they could heat their homes and cook their meals. He always had a smile on his lips and a kind word to say about everyone. So, when he died, he was sorely missed, not just by friends and family, but the whole parish.

Now for all that Simon was kindly and good hearted, his wife was mean and miserly; she was said to be a 'covetous, stingy old hag'. The moment her husband died she stopped making all payments to the poor. She wouldn't let them gather wood on her land, she wouldn't even pay the local priest his annual tithe, and the parish register of 23 June 1689 notes: 'Madame Benett gave nothing'. Everybody had to call her Madame. Oh, that Madame Bennett was mean. So mean that one day, to test her groundskeepers and make sure they were really keeping those terrible poor folk off her land, she disguised herself as a beggar woman and went to collect wood. Soon one of her groundskeepers saw her and came to stop the old beggar woman. Now the keeper was a quick fellow and realised who the old woman was straight away, but Madame Bennett was no kinder to her employees than she was to anyone else. So, he gave it the worst to her, beating and thrashing her, and the more she squealed and protested and told him who she was, the more he tormented her saying she shouldn't lie and surely, he would know his own mistress. If he had hoped this might make her kinder to the poor around her, then he was wrong.

Grace Bennett had, as they say, married up and now she didn't want anything to do with those in lower stations. Especially her family. She had a cousin called Adam Barnes who lived in Stony Stratford, where he was the local butcher. While Adam had fallen on hard times (some say of his own making) and so, needing some money urgently, he went to see his cousin Madame Bennett to plead for help.

It was the day of the Michaelmas hiring and horse fair in Stony Stratford, and the taverns had been busy. Madame Bennett didn't care for his drunkenness; his pleas fell on deaf ears, and she made it plain that she didn't want him coming back any more. A great argument began between the two of them and finally Adam went away fuming and empty-handed.

He made his way to one of the many taverns in Stony Stratford and set about drowning his sorrows, all the while complaining bitterly to all those who would listen about the terrible treatment he'd received from his snobbish cousin. As the ale flowed, it started to conjure an idea, an awful idea. An idea that would help him get even, an idea that might even allow him to get his hands on his cousin's money.

Later that evening, when all the celebrations in the town had settled and the pubs had turned everyone out, Adam went to pick up the tools of his trade and set off back to Calverton Manor farm.

Madame Bennett had a niece from her husband's side staying with her and, as it was late, the girl had already turned in for bed. Then, both the girl and Madame Bennett heard a great deal of clamour downstairs. The girl, in fright, ran to a nearby cottage near the church for help, but when she got back all the jewellery and family plate were gone – the place had been ransacked and in the middle of the mess lay Madame Bennett.

She had been properly butchered, with so much blood that it stained the flagstones, which could never be scrubbed clean. When the authorities arrived, the girl was in a terrible state, but she managed to tell them of the argument that had taken place earlier between Grace and Adam. Adam was arrested in Beechampton and in his possession were a few precious items that had been taken from the manor farm; this was enough.

Sometime after, the assizes were held upstairs in the Cross Keys public house on Stony Stratford High Street. And there Adam was found guilty and sentenced to death by hanging. He was taken to Gallows Hill to the south of Stony Stratford, a place now known by its much friendlier name of Galley Hill. There Adam was hung by the neck until he was dead, and because his crime had been so terrible, his body was placed in a gibbet, which was hung up in the lane stretching from Gallows Hill to Calverton, (now called Gibbs Lane). There, Adam was left until the birds had picked all the flesh from his bones, but even then, they didn't think he had suffered enough so his skull was taken and placed on a spike outside Manor Farm, just to remind any wrongdoers what might become of them if they crossed the line. Madame Bennett's ghost is said to still haunt the house.

## THE FENNY FORGER

*Long before Fenny Stratford existed, the ancient Roman fort of Magiovinium stood strong and imposing on the lands that had once belonged to the Catuvellauni tribe. Their new straight road Iber II (renamed by the Anglo–Saxons as Watling Street) cut through the area, and not even Boudicca's troops could take it back. But where there is power there is always someone trying to usurp it.*

Those damn Romans were everywhere; their roads cut through the land and their fortresses towered over the small homesteads of the Britons. Soldiers were everywhere, checking who went where and carrying what. But the trick was to work from the inside out, because that meant getting close, becoming familiar and going unseen.

That is what the Fenny Forger did. He got close enough to steal a stamp and forge a coin mould. He made hundreds of blank discs, which with one quick, firm stamp was suddenly imperial currency to be spent anywhere. From poor man to rich man overnight, oh how the Fenny Forger congratulated himself; why had no one done it before? It was so easy.

But becoming so rich so quick attracts attention … and questions. Soon soldiers were stopping him, searching his belongings, asking what he had bought, where had he got the money? Trouble was coming. He fobbed them off as quickly as possible and ran home to collect his coin mould and silver discs, and he ran to a hidden place and buried them deep, for when it was safe to return.

The days turned into weeks, which become months, which rolled into years, that stretched into centuries, and never did the Fenny Forger return to collect his tools. Perhaps he was caught, perhaps he had been scared into becoming honest, or maybe he simply forgot where he buried them. Whatever the reason, those silver discs and coin mould lay in the ground for 2,000 years.

The Romans had long since gone, leaving behind only their long straight road, which now cuts through the local village of Fenny Stratford. A new empire was coming to the area, that of Milton Keynes (bringing its straight grid roads), and Fenny Stratford needed a bypass as the heavy lorries thundered through the high street still using that ancient Iber II.

The diggers arrived but, like the rest of the new town of Milton Keynes, the archaeologists moved in first, and it was they who, after two millennia, discovered the hidden forgery equipment and revealed a story lost to the sands of time.

## THE SHOOTING PARTY

*There cannot be a collection of stories about Buckinghamshire without referring to one of the most famous places within its borders, Bletchley Park, where the hard work of the code breakers helped end the Second World War. There are many books about Bletchley Park and a visit to the museum that now occupies the site is well worth it. It wasn't until the 1970s that the remarkable stories of what went on at Bletchley Park came to light, but how did it start and what did the locals think?*

The Domesday Book mentions an estate on the very spot that the large Victorian mansion now stands, which makes sense as the name Bletchley comes from the Anglo–Saxon Blecca's Ley, or Blecca's (perhaps the local leader) clearing. Perhaps Blecca cleared the trees to make way for his grand home, little knowing that, one day, it would become the birthplace of modern-day computing.

In 1883, Sir Herbert Leon and his wife Fanny were looking for a new home to raise their family. Whilst hunting for their perfect home, they found Bletchley Park and decided that the hodgepodge of Victorian Gothic was just the place for them. Being avid travellers and fans of classical architecture, the Leons set about expanding the house by adding Roman columns here, and Grecian plasterwork there. To the passing eye, its dark woodwork and heavy architectural features may have been too gaudy for Edwardian tastes, which preferred a simpler more natural look, but the Leons loved it. They even decorated the nursery with lively Peter Rabbits leaping across the wall.

By the time Sir George Leon inherited the family home in 1937, he'd had quite enough of quiet country life and longed for adventure in the bright lights of the city. It didn't help that famed architectural chronicler Nikolaus Pevsner warned people against visiting Bletchley because its buildings were boring and had nothing to offer the refined eye. How rude!

So, George placed Bletchley Park up for sale. A small group of property developers, including Captain Faulkner, made a bid, but it was Admiral Sir Hugh Sinclair who paid for the house out of his own pocket. The admiral was a notable man, the head of MI6. What a fella to be neighbours with, thought the locals.

Of course, the people of Bletchley expected some changes, because everybody wants to make their new home their own. But soon after the purchase in May 1938, an army of post office engineers turned up and they started laying cables everywhere. One of those modern types, thought the locals; going to have all the mod cons.

But awe and maybe even a little envy gave way to scandal in August when a large group of 150 people, mainly older men and pretty young women, descended on the house. When some of the more curious locals enquired as to what was happening up at the big house, they were told it was 'Captain Ridley's Shooting Party'. There were so many of them that they booked up every bed and breakfast, hotel and hostel around Bletchley. Every day they would make their way up to the big house, and sometimes they wouldn't return to their lodgings until very late at night or even early the next morning. Funny thing was, they never seemed to go out shooting. It was scandalous! There was no telling what was going on up at that house, but with such rich men and such lovely ladies, it certainly set the gossips to work.

The cleaning staff at the many hotels got fed up with it too, all that coming and going. One maid remarked to one of the young ladies upon her comings and goings that she ought to be ashamed, and that it was causing a terrible strain on the staff, as 'some of us has to do work for a living!'

Obviously, the maid thought this young strumpet was avoiding work and being kept by her rich older lover.

But one day, as quickly as all the clamour had begun, the shooting party left and the town settled down, but the house did not. One wing was demolished, and soon huts were being erected all over its grounds, and then the people came, more and more with every train. Fancy young women, you could tell by their clothes and voices they were from well-to-do families, and smart men sometimes in casuals, sometimes in uniform.

In 1939 war broke out, the second great war began, and men of the town were called up. Yet, still men and women, especially women, began arriving in Bletchley. Soon, every bit of accommodation was taken, the government even had to requisition houses, and still the people came. Buses and special trains brought them in from other local towns and villages where they were billeted. Some walked, some rode their bicycles, like that strange chap staying at Shenley Brooke End who cycled in his gas mask.

It was obvious to the locals now that the government was using this big house as the centre of something important, but what? Some mused that the ladies must be nurses and it was surely a hospital for treating shellshock. Others thought that all the young men were 'conchies' (conscientious objectors) and were being imprisoned in those huts. Mad house or prison, the locals took some pride that they were in some way helping the war effort, and so the levels of secrecy that surrounded the park were also adopted by the town.

When the Second World War ended, Bletchley's soldiers received a hero's welcome home, while the park descended into quietness. It was to be another thirty years before the people of Bletchley discovered what had been going on on their very doorstep.

The Government Code and Cypher School had been set up in 1919 to monitor German and Soviet encrypted messages and, at the first signs of the impending war, the GC&CS had looked for somewhere safer than inner city Whitehall to expand and develop their operations. They chose Bletchley because of its direct train connected to London, Birmingham, Oxford and Cambridge. Running the operation was Commander Alistair Dennison, who took over from Sir Hugh Sinclair when he became very ill. Oh, and that little nursery with the rabbits on the wall, that became the office of Colonel John Tiltman. What secrets those bunnies must have heard!

# 4

# STORIES FROM THE STONY STORYTELLERS

*Before we conclude this book, we cannot do so without hearing a few words from the local storytelling group of Stony Stratford. I am pleased to say that these fine fellows have been learning the art of storytelling since 2015, and in that time have become fine tellers in their own right. In 2018, I challenged them to undertake a local folk tale project, by getting out into the landscape and to either (re)discover stories or create folk tales of some familiar place. This is the sort of project that I usually undertake with school children, but it is one that adults, given half a chance, also relish. What follows, therefore, are three of the stories created, because they illustrate that not all folk tales have to originate in the distant past to be worth the telling.*

# A LACEMAKER OR LUCKY GEMMA BY LYNETTE HILL

*It is widely believed that Flemish religious refugees brought the craft of lacemaking to England, and particularly to Buckinghamshire and the surrounding counties in the sixteenth century. In the 1880s a Stony Stratford lace school produced delicate butterfly-patterned lace to sell at markets in nearby Newport Pagnell and Buckingham. The old school was on the west side of the High Street, close to the site thought to be where Queen Eleanor's Cross stood.*

*Lacemaking was one of the few trades open to respectable women at the time, and it was often lauded as a way of keeping young women away from immorality. Girls (and some boys) were trained in the craft from the age of six. In good times, a female lacemaker could earn more than a male agricultural labourer. Lacemakers often worked ten to twelve hours a day at this repetitive task and would chant 'tells' like, 'Jack be nimble, Jack be quick, Jack jumped over a candlestick,' to help keep their place in the pattern.*

Everyone said that Gemma was lucky when she got that job as a shop assistant at that London department store. And she felt lucky, too, that very first week when smooth-talking Johnny started taking her around to see the sights. It wasn't until a month after he left for his ship, that sharp-eyed Mrs Slocombe, Gemma's manager, noticed her bump and explained to naive young Gemma exactly why she kept being sick in the mornings.

But even then, it seemed that Gemma's luck held. Instead of sacking her, Mrs Slocombe said she'd been young once too and invited Gemma to move in with her. She showed Gemma how to dress to hide that bump and got her assigned to the deliveries department in the back of the store, away from the prying eyes of overly observant customers. When the pains came, Mrs Slocombe called the midwife for her – 'the good one,' Mrs Slocombe said; 'the one that really knows what she's doing.'

They said Gemma was lucky the birth happened so quickly. She heard the sound of the slap on the baby's bottom and its loud cry. When Gemma held out her arms and asked, 'Please, let me hold my baby?' the midwife said, 'Just a minute' and gave her something that tasted like medicine to drink.

'For the bleeding,' the midwife said.

When Gemma woke up again all fuzzy headed, it seemed that all of her luck had vanished, along with her baby.

Mrs Slocombe told her the baby was dead; that the baby had been born dead, bless him.

'But I heard it cry,' Gemma protested. 'A loud, healthy cry.'

She argued so much that Mrs Slocombe called her an ungrateful slut and threw her out onto the street with nothing more than the clothes she wore.

Still aching from the birth and dizzy from the drink, Gemma walked the streets of London in a daze. She walked for hours, uncertain what to do. But as her mind cleared, she became more and more certain of a number of things.

She had given birth to a healthy, living child. Only a healthy child could give out such a loud cry.

And she remembered that, as she had felt herself falling asleep from that drink, she'd heard Mrs Slocombe and the midwife laughing.

'Oh, they'll pay handsomely for him,' one of them had said. And then something about a couple named Jenkins in a place called Stony Stratford.

Gemma found herself standing in front of Euston Station. She went inside and asked the ticket seller if he knew where Stony Stratford was, and if the train went there. It didn't, not directly, and Gemma didn't have any money for a ticket anyway. But she was determined that she would get there.

I can't tell you all of the ways that Gemma took to get herself to Stony Stratford, but in a couple of days she stood at the corner of the London and Wolverton Roads, in the middle of town.

'Will you be all right, Miss?' asked the kindly farmer, who had given her a lift on his cart the last couple of miles to town.

Gemma assured him that she would be, and then turned to see herself in the reflection of a large shop window. Her shoes and dress were filthy with mud, her hair a wild bird's nest, her face drawn and pale. To see her anyone would think she was mad; and they just might be right. As dusk fell, she walked hesitantly up London Road, uncertain what to do next.

And then, it seemed, she got lucky again. A woman stepped out of the shadows and greeted her. It was Meg. You know, *that* Meg. Good Time Meg. If the women of Stony Stratford didn't know her, well, all of the men certainly did.

She invited Gemma to come to her place for a meal and a bath and a bed. There, some of the other women who lived there drew her a bath and helped wash her clothes and hair. Meg gave Gemma her first real meal in two days, and then a soft bed in a warm corner. Gemma was asleep before her head hit the pillow.

The next morning Meg gave Gemma a choice.

'I won't have a girl in this house who doesn't enjoy her work,' Meg said.

And so Gemma went back to her old trade, the one she'd learned as a child in her village, the one she'd thought she'd put aside forever when she got that job at the London department store. Gemma joined the lace-makers of Stony Stratford.

In good weather, to get the best light, the lace-makers sat under the old oak tree on the north side of town, near to where people think the old Eleanor Cross stood.

'A tisket, a tasket, a green and yellow basket,' Gemma and the other lace-makers chanted to keep the count as they twisted the thread and moved the pins to make the butterfly lace that once made Stony Stratford famous.

From there, under the tree, Gemma could sit in such a way that she could see the front door to the Jennings house. Mr Jennings was an engineer at the nearby Watling Works. According to Meg and others, theirs was the only house in Stony Stratford to announce a happy delivery the day before Gemma arrived.

But how could she be certain this was her child? She hadn't held it, hadn't even seen it. Gemma worried about this until the day when Mrs Jennings and the nursemaid stepped out of their house proudly carrying a bundle well wrapped up in swaddling clothes. The child gave a heart-stopping cry and Gemma's heart expanded with joy at the sound. *Yes*, this was her child.

The Jennings named him Edward.

A young woman named Annie, who happened to be the same age as Gemma, was his nursemaid.

Gemma made it her business to become very good friends indeed with Annie; and with Joe, the Jennings' gardener, and with the other members of their household. When Annie gave notice about a year later when her young man finally popped the question, it seemed only natural that Gemma should be hired in her place. And then, finally, Gemma could hold her child, and dress him and comb his hair and tell him stories at night before tucking him into bed.

She very nearly bolted with him that first day; only the hard-won patience she'd learned over the past year kept her there. She did not yet have her own place; the little cottage she dreamed of that would have enough of a garden for veg-etables and perhaps even a goat; a place where a healthy little boy would have room to run and play.

And there were definitely advantages to staying with the Jennings for a time. When little Edward took ill, the doctor turned up as soon as Mrs Jennings sent for him. On cold days there was always coal in the fire to keep everyone warm; even Gemma and the other servants. There was plenty of good food at every meal and Edward always had the best clothes to wear. It turned a dagger in her heart every time Edward called Mrs Jennings 'mother' as he grew older. Of course, it did. On those days she counted her savings and dreamed of the little house and reminded herself, as time passed, that her son now had a tutor and was getting a real education.

When Edward turned nine years old, Mr Jennings declared that it was time to stop 'coddling the boy' and send him off to boarding school. Gemma bit down hard on her own tongue as Mrs Jennings argued with her husband.

'Edward's too young, dear. Perhaps in another year …'

But Mr Jennings was adamant. His son already had a place reserved at Oxford and he needed to be properly prepared for that. The uniforms were already on order.

Gemma helped Edward dress in his new finery and took him down to the living room to show him off to Mrs Jennings and the rest of the household.

And that's when it happened.

Gemma reached over to brush a bit of lint off Edward's shoulder. She heard Mrs Jennings gasp. And whether it was a trick of the light or the turn of a head, Gemma didn't know, but when she glanced up, Mrs Jennings was looking from Edward's face to hers and back again.

In a falsely cheerful voice, Mrs Jennings said, 'Edward, that's lovely. Why don't you go to the kitchen and show Cook?'

As Edward dashed off, Gemma stood up very straight and looked Mrs Jennings right in the eye. She waited until she was certain that the boy was out of earshot before speaking.

'Shall I go pack my things, madam?'

'Please,' Mrs Jennings indicated the seat next to hers. 'Sit down and tell me your story.'

Now I can't tell you what those two women said to each other in the very long conversation that followed, but I can tell you this. When Edward graduated from Oxford, sadly

Mr Jennings had already passed away. But Edward could still look out across the audience to see his mother, Mrs Alicia Jennings, sitting shoulder to shoulder with his mother, Miss Gemma Whitley, together in celebration of his accomplishments.

## CURLY KALE AND QUINOA BY PHIL CHIPPENDALE

*The story is based on the Brothers Grimm folk tale 'Cat and Mouse in Partnership'. I adapted it to set it in Stony Stratford. I had recently been asked to write a poem on the subject of the Magdalen Tower, so it was fresh in my mind, and changing the name to 'Mary Mogg's' seemed a useful joke to support the story. Also, I once considered moving to Temperance Terrace, and the name seemed appropriate for the mouse's character. The story was developed through a process of improvisation, changing different aspects of the original Grimm tale over several retellings, before eventually producing a written version.*

Once upon a time in Stony Stratford, there was a cat who made friends with a mouse. They set up house together in a desirable residence with a cat flap, in Temperance Terrace, overlooking the water meadows by the river, facing away from the various temptations of the town of Stony Stratford. This was good because it was a homely little mouse, happy to avoid busy places.

They decided to provide for the future by purchasing a pot of fat, to see them through the winter, when it inevitably arrived.

But where should they put it for safekeeping?

Eventually they decided the best place would be in the former church of St Mary Magdalen's haunted tower, on the east side of the town, behind the High Street, sometimes called 'St. Mary Mag's'.

'Mary Mog's, as I like to call it,' said the cat.

'You'll have to give up your stupid puns if we're to live together,' said the mouse. 'Furthermore, I'll be setting the menu at home. My favourite dish is curly kale and quinoa.'

The cat agreed to the mouse's terms, but, before long, the cat became fed up with curly kale and quinoa and began to think about the pot of fat in Mary Mog's tower.

'Curly kale and quinoa aren't fit for a kitten,' said the cat.

Therefore, the cat invented a cousin who had given birth to a little kitten.

'It's grey all over. I have to go, I've been invited to be a godparent,' said the cat. 'It's far away though, it's near the end of the Earth; go any further and you fall off the edge. It's a place called Horsefair Green. It's far too far for you and your little legs,' said the cat. The mouse agreed.

'But bring me something from the christening, perhaps a little wine,' said the mouse.

Instead of going to Horsefair Green, the cat sneaked directly to Mary Mog's, opened the pot of fat, and licked the top off the fat. Then the cat took a stroll along the high street, and feeling nicely satisfied, climbed on to the roofs to sunbathe. In the evening, the cat went back home to Temperance Terrace and the mouse.

'Did you bring me anything from the christening?' asked the mouse.

'Sorry, forgot!' replied the cat.

'Never mind. But what was your new godchild called?'

'Topoff,' replied the cat.

'Topoff! What a funny name!' said the mouse.

'That's what they called it,' said the cat.

Before long, the cat began to yearn for the pot of fat again, so another cousin was invented, and another new kitten.

'I'll have to go, this one is marmalade coloured with black socks, very unusual,' explained the cat. The cat headed directly for St Mary Mog's again, and to the pot of fat.

Opening the pot, the cat licked the fat until it was half eaten.

Feeling satisfied, the cat took a stroll along the high street and curled up in a nice warm spot on the Cock Hotel for a nap.

In the evening, the cat returned.

'What is this one called?' asked the mouse.

'Halfdone,' replied the cat.

'Halfdone?' 'Halfdone!' What a strange name! It's very disturbing!' said the mouse.

'It's no worse than your family. They're all called Crumbstealer. Crumbstealer junior, Crumbstealer the third, Crumbstealer 150th, etc.'

'Okay, no need to go on about it,' said the mouse. 'Besides, I've got good news for you. I'm changing the menu. From now on, it's curly kale and couscous.'

'Curly kale and couscous aren't fit for a puss puss,' muttered the cat.

The cat began to yearn for the pot of fat again, so another cousin was invented, with another newborn kitten.

'This one is brown with pink spots,' said the cat. It's possible the cat was running out of ideas. 'It's a very rare combination; my cousin will never forgive me if I don't go.'

Once again the cat went straight to Mary Mog's and the pot of fat. Opening the pot, the cat licked the fat until the pot was empty.

Then the cat took a stroll along the high street and napped on the roof of the Bull Hotel, returning late at night.

'How was the christening?' asked the mouse.

'Excellent,' said the cat. 'The kitten was called Allgone'.

'Allgone!' said the mouse. 'That name is even more worrying than the others!'

With the pot of fat empty, there was no point in the cat thinking about it anymore.

When winter came, however, the mouse's thoughts turned to the pot of fat in St Magdalen's Tower.

'Let's go to St Magdalen's Tower and fetch the pot of fat,' said the mouse.

'You'll be lucky,' said the cat.

They arrived, and to the mouse's dismay, the pot was empty.

'I see it all now. Top off! Half done! All gone! They were just excuses for you to eat the fat.'

'One more word and I'll eat you too!' said the cat.

'You lied!' said the mouse, whereupon the cat pounced and ate the mouse whole.

'I'm never eating curly kale or quinoa ever again,' said the cat.


## JIM AND MABEL BY STEPHEN HOBBS

*In 2017 I was invited as Bard of Stony Stratford to do a Christmas 'turn' for the staff of Willen Hospice Bookshop. I was very happy to do so as I knew many of them; indeed, I was always in there buying books! Afterwards, over a cup of tea and a cucumber sandwich, a lady said, 'May I tell you a story? It's the story of how my parents met.'*

*And this is how 'Jim and Mabel' began. I made a few notes. I was also able to question my source. What sort of bicycles? What did they eat? What did they wear? How rarely do you get the chance to do this? So, when a mural was painted in Stony Stratford of Queen Eleanor (Edward Longshanks' Queen) I thought it perfectly fitting that I should pay my own tribute to Jim and Mabel, and even more delighted that it should appear in a book.*

Now here's a love story! It's not *Romeo and Juliet*; it's not Edward IV and Elizabeth Woodville; it's not even Edward I and Queen Eleanor. It's the story of Jim and Mabel. You've probably not heard of them – how could you? They have no Shakespeare, no statues, and no schools named after them; but they're still worthy of your attention.

Let me introduce them to you. Here's Jim, a twenty-year-old apprentice engineer from Birmingham: he wipes his hands down his trouser legs and shakes your hand. 'Howdoo,' he says. Here's Mabel, a nineteen-year-old ladies' maid at a big fine London house: she straightens her pinafore and bobs her head. 'Pleased to meet you I'm sure,' she says.

Anyone can see that they're perfect for each other, but under normal life it's impossible that they will ever meet. Birmingham? London? They live in different worlds, and it's the 1920s and most people still live, work, marry and die close to home. So, fate must intervene if they are ever to meet; and of course, she does, as a very distant relative to both of them dies and they're invited to the funeral. The distant relative is a lady of venerable age, a lady who had had a good innings: so, the funeral is not a sombre event, but a celebration of a life well lived; and there are a great many people there to share the farewell, many themselves quite elderly.

Jim and Mabel are by far the youngest there, so it's not surprising that they should find themselves sitting in the same pew in the church; or that they are next to each other in the queue for a cup of tea; or indeed that their elbows should touch as they sit to drink their tea and eat their cucumber sandwiches with the crusts cut off. They introduce themselves and begin to talk. They discover that not only do they have the distant relative in common, but also that they are both keen cyclists. Not just the odd mile or two popping down to the shops, but real journeys of ten or twenty miles! And, they both own Claud Butler bicycles!

Claud Butler bikes are the very latest, known only in the largest cities. Their eponymous designer was the James Dyson of his time; whilst most people cycled around on Hoovers, a discerning few went for the Claud Butlers. There was definitely something about them (not just the three gears that came as standard) and that something was style. His bicycles just looked so stylish. Indeed, a Claud Butler was guaranteed to turn heads, and those who rode them never went back to other bicycles. They were proud of their CBs, as they called them.

Jim and Mabel spent the afternoon talking about their CBs and the journeys they had made; and when it was time to leave, they realised that they wanted to see each other again. But times were hard and neither of them earned enough to make long journeys on public transport.

'We could just wait until the next funeral,' Mabel suggested with a laugh.

'Mmm, I've a better idea,' said Jim as he reached into his jacket pocket and took out a well-worn Ordnance Survey map, a constant friend that he always carried, even to funerals. He spread it out on a table and opened the top and bottom panels.

'Here's me,' he said, pointing to Birmingham, 'and here's you,' pointing to London.

'This road here, the A5, practically joins us up. There's a bit of a dog leg near me, but it's pretty much a straight line.'

Mabel leaned forward and then she placed her finger on the map.

'Here's halfway. We could meet up here? This could be our rendezvous?'

Jim leaned forward, placing his finger next to hers on the map.

'I think you're right,' he said, 'but it'll mean a bike journey of two and a half hours and that's just one way. Is this something you can do, lass?'

Mabel smiled, 'I can if you can, lad,' she said.

So, on their very next day off, Jim and Mabel set off on their CBs. Jim south-east from Birmingham, and Mabel northwest from London, and after a two-and-a-half-hour journey they met up at the town of Rendezvous. That was their very first date, the day they started walking out (cycling out really) together. And this was their courtship for the next five years. Mabel brought sandwiches, usually cheese, and Jim brought fruit. Sometimes they would even pop in to a public house to buy a fizzy Vimto, which they would share as they cycled around. And they did turn heads, these two young happy people on their Claud Butler cycles; and even a few wagging fingers, because Mabel insisted on wearing trousers. Long skirts were so impracticable! Jim loved her even more.

Now the town of Rendezvous is not like it is today, a rather quiet town. In the 1920s, there was no bypass and the M1 motorway was thirty years away. Then, all the traffic between Birmingham and London thundered down the A5 and you had to have your wits about you just to cross the high street. The Leylands, the Bedfords, the Fodens, and all those heritage lorries that paid little heed to pedestrians or cyclists. There's a lovely story about two old men seeing their pal Turnip across the high street and try as they might they just could not get across to him.

Turning to his friend, one said, 'How on earth did Turnip get across that road?'

'Ah,' said his friend, 'Turnip were born that side of the road.'

One day Jim turned up to Rendezvous with his arm in plaster and a sling! I'd love to be able to tell you that it was after a collision with a tram; because then I could tell you about the mighty tram of Rendezvous. A tram so big – the biggest in the world some said – it could carry 100 men from Rendezvous to a nearby engineering works. But that's not what happened, so I can't tell you that story. It actually happened in Birmingham, where Jim was a little careless and the front wheel of his CB got caught in a tram line and he was flicked over his handlebars and broke his arm. But he got himself up, had his arm set in plaster, made himself a sling and set off to Rendezvous. For the next two months he continued to make that journey despite his discomfort.

Five years later, Jim completed his apprenticeship and felt able to propose to Mabel. I like to think he got off his Claud Butler to propose, but I couldn't be sure. Mabel accepted, but when they started to look for a little house in Birmingham there was nothing they could afford. Mabel's employer had a suggestion. Of course, Mabel should marry her young man but couldn't they both live in their gatehouse? I told you it was a big fine London house. Jim could be their chauffeur and handyman? They would also keep Mabel who, in the past five years, had risen from ladies' maid to head housekeeper – a position of some importance. This suited everyone, so by the time the children came along, Jim and Mabel were able to buy that small house in Birmingham.

Jim's new engineering job kept him very busy, but they were still seen out and about on their CB bikes. In fact, when Claud Butler brought out a tandem, Jim and Mabel were one of the first people to buy one; and they even had it specially adapted so that there was a child's seat in the middle between Jim and Mabel.

Jim and Mabel's family thrived, even during the Second World War when Birmingham was in the front line as Britain's major manufacturing city. Jim's engineering skills were vital to the war effort and they kept him at home; but at night he was an air raid precautions warden. After the war, life became a little easier and their two children grew up and left home to start their own lives. Some years later, in the 1960s, their daughter introduced them to her young man. He had prospects, and had just got a wonderful new job in a new town they were building alongside the M1: a place called Milton Keynes.

Jim and Mabel couldn't be happier for the young people, even if it meant them moving away from Birmingham, going to Milton Keynes and buying a house in a nearby town called Stony Stratford. They were invited to visit and they were driven down the M1 to view their daughter's new home.

It was a lovely warm day as they sat in the garden drinking tea and eating cucumber sandwiches with the crusts cut off. Jim got up to stretch his legs, and he walked down the garden and looked over the hedge at the bottom of the garden. Suddenly, he started shouting and waving his arms at Mabel. Mabel rushed to his side and soon she too was waving her arms. Their daughter and son-in-law were perplexed.

'Look,' said Jim pointing over the hedge, 'There is the very spot where your mother and I used to rendezvous all those years ago.' The town of Rendezvous was Stony Stratford!

Now, I know that this story is not *Romeo and Juliet*; it's not Edward IV and Elizabeth Woodville; and it's not Edward I and Queen Eleanor. For Jim and Mabel there is no Shakespeare, no statues, and no schools named after them; but their story is part of the living heritage of Stony Stratford. The story of Jim and Mabel is the story of ordinary people; it is the story of us.

## Once Upon a Milton Keynes by Terrie Howey

*Whilst finding stories about Milton Keynes for my PhD, I became more and more confused why there is such a widely held belief that Milton Keynes seems to lack cultural heritage. As part of my PhD studies I took these stories of history, urban myths, personal tales and, of course, folk tales to various areas within Milton Keynes in the form of a storytelling performance. I ended the performance with a short story I created in the style of a folk tale that encapsulated the situation, so I feel it is fitting to conclude this collection with the same story. Folk tales are not some distant narrative created by forgotten tellers, they are our stories, created and shared by us all the time.*

Have you heard the joke, 'What is the difference between Milton Keynes and a yoghurt?

A yoghurt has culture!'

Once upon a time, there were too many people and not enough houses (sounds familiar doesn't it), so the government decided to build new towns and the last one they built was the biggest and most successful, and they called it Milton Keynes. Thousands of people migrated there from all over the country and even the world, it was the 'city of dreams'.

The houses were new, the people were new; everything was new. At first, Milton Keynes sparkled in its newness, but then the other towns and cities began to laugh at its roundabouts, its glass and its concrete. They said it was less of a place because it had no culture or heritage.

'Even a yoghurt has culture,' they laughed. So, when Milton Keynes celebrated its fiftieth birthday, it thought, 'Now I'm not so young, surely people will like me better!' but the residents still joked and the older towns, villages and cities still laughed.

But, by chance, a passing storyteller heard these jokes. Yet, wherever she looked she saw stories peeking out from here and there, their hiding places unseen by residents too busy to notice. She heard the whispered voices of Milton Keynes and began a quest discovering folk tales of witches and highwaymen, histories of kings and queens, and urban myths of roundabouts, coffee cups and town plans. Milton Keynes was brimming with stories; it did have a heritage after all.

The storyteller found many stories that were waiting for people to tell them. So, she showed the people of Milton Keynes where to find the stories, saying, 'We are all storytellers, and therefore the curators of the heritage we tell and pass on.' Now the people became the storytellers, sharing their past and making new stories for the future, because everyone knew that the difference between Milton Keynes and a yoghurt is that Milton Keynes has stories and therefore heritage.

# Notes on Stories

## South Buckinghamshire Stories

*Ghosties Don't Like Iron*
Area: Prestwood
Date: 1938
It is a well-known folklore tradition that the fey folk (fairies, elves, imps, trolls and goblins) and some demons can be repelled by iron, and it was also believed that a witch's power could be undone by iron. This story extends the belief that iron is also a source of protection against ghosts. Why iron should be so effective against supernatural forces is believed to relate to how useful iron proved itself to be once people learnt how to make iron weapons. There are plenty of stories of smithies having extra powers by extension of their skill to turn rock into metal –a real life feat of magic in bygone days. This story is dated as being collected in 1938, however the Women's Land Army movement did not begin until June 1939; perhaps the date given here is when the women telling the story to Tongue heard it, or perhaps it is a clerical error.
Sources: Tongue, R., 1970.

## The Vampire of Buckinghamshire

Area: Undisclosed village in Buckinghamshire
Date: 1192

The term vampire didn't come into use until the eighteenth century when people such as Bram Stoker made it famous with his book *Dracula* in 1897. Before him, John Polidori wrote *The Vampyre* in 1819, which was itself based upon Lady Caroline Lamb's story *Glenarvon* in 1816; this styled the vampire on real-life poet and noble rebel Lord Byron.
Sources: Topham, 2012; George, 2018; Occult-Media, 2018.

## The Poacher

Area: Throughout Buckinghamshire
Date: 1600s–1700s

The song of the poacher has been sung around the county for at least the last century and probably longer. It has been heard in Gawcott to Milton Keynes and would have been popular with anyone from the working classes who had their rights to hunt stopped by the enclosures. Although there were strict laws on poaching, including being transported or executed, the poacher became a hero figure who attracted the sympathies of the common folk, almost like a local Robin Hood, in stealing from the rich to feed the poor.
Sources: Word of mouth/local folk song (Harman, 1934; Archer, 1987; Piper, 1996).

## Witch's Stone Treasure – Nanny Copper & The Highwayman

Area: Speen
Date: Pre-eighteenth century, possibly pre-Civil War.

This story appeared on a geocaching website, with a further note from a local resident giving more details.

However, many who went looking for the stones as part of the geocaching activity failed to find it, so perhaps the ghosts have taken to hiding the treasure these days rather than trying to scare people off.

The Tyburn Jig was the nickname given to hanging, as the victim's legs would thrash about, looking like they were dancing a jig in the air. Tyburn, an area of London, was a famous execution ground with multiple gibbets for hanging the condemned.

Sources: Geocaching, 2003.

### ... And More Highwaymen

Area: Throughout Buckinghamshire and Edlesborough
Date: Late 1600s–1800s.

Claude Duvall is reputed to have come to Buckinghamshire on several occasions, and on one occasion so terrified a group of travellers with tales of highwaymen that when he held up the wealthy farmer there was no protest. The tales shared here were not the stories Claude would have told, as there are, admittedly, some time discrepancies between Claude and the other highwaymen. However, with so many highwaymen in Buckinghamshire it made for a useful device to share so many stories in a concise way, else the book would be made up mostly of highwaymen.

Claude was eventually caught, and at his trial it was said the great and the good of female aristocracy turned out to plead for his release. But his former master, Charles II, wanted to stamp out highway robbery, and so upheld his strict policy of death to all highwaymen. Claude was taken to Tyburn to dance the jig in January 1670, and afterwards it was said those noble ladies paid for his grave to be placed in the central aisle of St Paul's in Covent Garden where his epitaph reads:

Here lies DuVall: Reder, if male thou art,
Look to thy purse; if female, to thy heart.
Much havoc has he made of both; for all
Men he made to stand, and women he made to fall
The second Conqueror of the Norman race,
Knights to his arm did yield, and ladies to his face.
Old Tyburn's glory; England's illustrious Thief,
Du Vall, the ladies' joy; Du Vall, the ladies' grief.

Sources: *The Bucks Free Press*, 1882; Uttley, 1950; Topham, 2015; Editors of Encyclopaedia Britannica, 2019.

## The Water's Warning
Area: Great Missenden
Date: 1939

This story was reportedly collected by Ruth Tongue in 1939, however the Blitz did not begin until the early evening on 7 September 1940, so the collection date of this story might be a clerical error. Around 350 bombers dropped 300 tonnes of bombs on London in that first attack and continued for more than fifty nights without pause. Not just London but Liverpool, Bristol, Cambridge and Coventry were also targeted.
Sources: *The Bucks Free Press*, 1882; Tongue, R., 1970; Lucas, 1993.

## Dragon's Pond
Area: Hughendon
Date: 1578

Hughendon was once named Hitchendon. The house mentioned in the story was once a hospital for the Knights Templar and sits about half a mile from the church, where many Templars are buried. The painting mentioned in the story at the end is notably stated to have been repainted by Rowell in 1710, who added wings and legs to the water serpent, giving it a much more dragon-like appearance.

Sources: Catalog Record: *The Gentleman's Magazine,* Hathi Trust Digital Library, 1758; The Gentleman's Magazine archives, n.d.

## The Green Man of Fingest

Area: Fingest

Date: 1330

Some say the Green Man is linked to the Celtic God Cernunnos or Herne the Hunter (a ghost who appears in Windsor Forest), since both appear in legends about the Wild Hunt, and seeing the Wild Hunt is regarded as a bad omen. Often the Wild Hunt is accompanied by a pack of hounds – ghostly black dogs, of which there have been numerous sightings around Buckinghamshire throughout the years; some accounts can be found in these pages. Some say the Green Man appears on a ley line that runs through the area and is connected to the Dragon Pond at Princes Risborough and the Witch's Stone at Speen – both stories can be found in this volume. There are also stories from Swanbourne detailing a Green Lady, the reputed ghost of Elizabeth Adams, whose husband Thomas was mugged and murdered. She never quite got over it, visiting his grave in the churchyard every evening after she had put their four children to bed. When the children were grown, Elizabeth simply passed from this life, but has still been seen dressed all in green on many an evening walking along the road to the church.

Sources: Uttley, 1950; Archer, 1989; Lucas, 1993; Houghton, 1994; Hartland, 2000; Matthews, 2004; Kidd-Hewitt, 2008; Topham, 2015; Dancer, 2016.

## The Church Mystery

Area: West Wycombe

Date: Unknown

The church has received much interest over the years because of its connection to the Hellfire Club and the potential sinful activities that took place in the golden ball Sir Francis had built on the top of it. Many people at the time of its construction disliked it for they felt it made the church look ungodly. It is also interesting to note that the cave system of the Hellfire Club is built into the hill upon where the church sits, and that the original site picked for the church was supposed to be where the caves entrance is now. The main temple chamber of the cave network was constructed directly under the church. The church itself is built from the flint dug out from the early cave; perhaps this is why they wanted to build it at the bottom of the hill – so they didn't need to carry it up to the top.

Sources: *The Bucks Free Press*, 1882; Uttley, 1950; Lucas, 1993; Houghton, 1994; Kidd-Hewitt, 2008.

## Mad Monks of Medmenham

Area: West Wycombe & Medmenham

Date: 1745

Sir Francis and the Hellfire Club truly divide historians, some believing the stories of unholy acts, other viewing it as a bit of fun between consenting adults. I have tried as much as possible in the retelling of this history to be as neutral as possible and leave the reader to make up their own mind or, if they wish, to do further research. Whatever the varying views upon the club, it is undeniable that the Hellfire is perhaps one of the most famous stories to come from Buckinghamshire and therefore justly deserves a mention in this volume.

Sources: *The Bucks Free Press*, 1882; Uttley, 1950; Hippisley Coxe, 1973; Archer, 1987; Lucas, 1993; Houghton, 1994; Matthews, 2004; Kidd-Hewitt, 2008.

## Sukie's Love

Area: West Wycombe

Date: 1745–65

As with many folk tales, there are many versions of Sukie's story. Some say she was left for dead at the caves, others that the boys sneaked her back into her bed or took her back to the George and Dragon to seek help, but it was, alas, too late. Whatever her actual fate, the rest of the story is agreed by many versions and gives us a better understanding of what (at least) some of the locals thought of the Hellfire Club in its day. Sources: Hippisley Coxe, 1973; Matthews, 2004; Kidd-Hewitt, 2008; Dancer, 2016.

## The Amersham Martyrs

Area: Amersham

Date: 1511–32

The first Martyrs from Amersham to be burnt were Richard Turner, Walter Young and John Horwood in 1414.

Sources: *The Bucks Free Press*, 1882; Uttley, 1950; Hallam, 1972; Archer, 1989; Lucas, 1993; Bucks Free Press and Andrews-Reading, 2004; Matthews, 2004; Westwood and Simpson, 2005; Amersham musuem, 2016; Dancer, 2016.

## Denizens of Another World

Area: High Wycombe

Date: 4 October 1871

The strange lights in the sky could be put down to the night fever William was suffering from, but it is the strange craft he found the next day that really adds a twist to the tale.

Sources: Lucas, 1993.

## Bull Riders

Area: Bulstrode, Gerrards Cross

Date: 1067 or thereafter

This story has a touch of wonder about it: the Anglo-Saxon lord tames the beast and wins the day. In truth, historians now believe the earthwork found in Bulstrode Park is most likely Iron Age and not Anglo-Saxon. However, there is no reason why Shobbington would not have utilised the defences of a former age in his battle to save his lands.

Sources: *The Bucks Free Press*, 1882; Archer, 1989; Briggs, 1991; Lucas, 1993; Westwood and Simpson, 2005.

## Don't Eat the Stew!

Area: Colnbrook

Date: 1100–35

This story comes from Thomas Deloney's *Thomas of Reading: or the sixe worthy yeomen of the west*, which tells the fate of the six clothiers from the West Country. It is a deeply complex tale, covering not just the six clothiers but also the struggle of King Henry as he dealt with his rebellious older brother, Robert Duke of Normandy, who believed he had a stronger claim to the throne of England. Throughout there are also plenty of twists and love stories, but what is presented here follows just a small piece of the tale.

In the story, the tavern is referred to as the Crane but in reality, as far as records show, the tavern was always called the Ostrich. Perhaps a missing reading of the bird on the sign caused Deloney some confusion, or perhaps he changed the name to try and protect the owners – who can say.

Source: Deloney, 1632; *The Bucks Free Press*, 1882; Briggs, 1991; Woodley, 2009.

## The Raven's Curse
Area: West Drayton
Date: Unknown
With the re-drawing of county lines in the 1970s, Buckinghamshire lost part of its southern territory to Berkshire. Originally West Drayton, Slough, and Eton were all considered parts of Buckinghamshire, and whilst researching this book I came across some wonderful stories from the old county. The other stories I left out with a hope that the authors of the other counties will find them, but this story was just too engaging, so I hope you will permit me to steal back a piece of Buckinghamshire heritage.
Sources: Westwood and Simpson, 2005.

## STORIES FROM NORTH BUCKINGHAMSHIRE

### Dr Allen's Familiar
Area: Thornton
Date: 1630
This tale was discovered by Houghton in a brief note in the Thornton parish records, but the account was intriguing enough to construct the full story.
Sources: Houghton, 1995; Smith, 2018.

### The Earl's Fox
Area: Aylesbury Vale
Date: Unknown
This story is an amalgamation of two fox stories and a poem, 'The Captive Fox', as recounted in J.K. Fowler's *Echoes of Old Country Life and Recollections of Old Country Life*.
Sources: Fowler, 1892, 1894.

## Wingrave Witches

Area: Wingrave

Date: Unknown (sometime between 1643 and after 1726)

Witchfinders would often use a 'witch prick' – a pointy needle used to pierce any marks (moles, bruises, or large freckles) on the body that witchfinders claimed were the devil's teat, where Satan would suckle from the witches. They believed the prick could pierce these marks and not cause bleeding, and so accused witches were prodded and poked, often with hidden retractable needles because the witchfinders got paid by the number of witches they successfully dispatched. These witches would have their heads shaved, their clothes taken from them, and a common way of securing a confession was to 'walk the witch' sometimes for days, pushing the witch to keep walking, never sleeping or eating, not even stopping to relieve themselves. Soon the accused was so delirious that they would agree to anything: of course they had danced with the devil; yes, they can fly; and with often little more than a 'X', their confession was signed.

In England, confessed witches were often put through a trial. They could be ducked (submerged in water: if they drowned it showed their soul was innocent and could enter heaven; if they floated they were a witch – sadly, due to air getting trapped in the layers of ladies petticoats, on occasion they did float), weighed (usually against a feather or the Bible – it was believed that, due to their unholy nature, witches were as light as air), or by iron bar (they had to hold a red-hot iron bar; if the wound healed cleanly they were innocent, if it festered it showed their festering soul).

Sources: *The Bucks Free Press*, 1882; Houghton, 1995, 2000.

### The Witch's Hurdle
Area: Bishopstone
Date: Unknown
This tale needed very little work, as the original taken down in the Buckinghamshire dialect is beautiful. I heartily recommend anyone interested in this county finds a copy and discovers its wonders for themselves.
Source: Harman, 1934; Westwood and Simpson, 2005.

### A Stare as Hard as Stone
Area: Stone
Date: Unknown
*See notes above for Witch's Hurdle.*
Sources: Harman, 1934; Westwood and Simpson, 2005.

### The Little Witches
Area: Eythrope
Date: Unknown
Like the other two stories from the Buckinghamshire Triangle, I heartily recommend reading Harman's original version. I was so enamoured of the dialect version I was sorely tempted to include it in this volume. However, for accessibility, I chose to retell the story, but have used a touch of accent to the speech of the watchman instead.
Sources: Harman, 1934; Westwood and Simpson, 2005.

### Wendover Witches
Area: Wendover
Date: Unknown
There are many instances of moving churches; in Buckinghamshire there are moving churches in Olney and Ibstone, as well as the two other examples included in the book from Stowe and West Wycombe.

Sources: *The Bucks Free Press*, 1882; Uttley, 1950; Houghton, 1994.

## Stowe-away Church

Area: Stowe

Date: Unknown

It was said the lord of the manor had an issue with the placement of the church; perhaps this offers a more man-made reason why it kept moving.

Sources: *The Bucks Free Press*, 1882; Houghton, 1994.

## The Quainton Thorn

Area: Quainton

Date: 1752

This is not the only miracle thorn descended from the Glastonbury thorn in Buckinghamshire. In the new town of Milton Keynes, one of the thirteen original villages, Shenley Church End had another holy thorn tree, now surrounded by railings near the playground on Holy Thorn Lane. The *Wolverton Express* (now the *Citizen* newspaper) reported in 1963 that 'some who made the journey for the first were very sceptical until they actually saw the tree in bloom'.

There is another story from Quainton about poor souls who have encountered a headless horseman who rides through the lanes in the dead of night, only announcing his presence by the clatter of invisible hooves until he shows himself in his full 'gory'.

Sources: Shenley Church End Parish Council, no date; Uttley, 1950; *Wolverton Express*, 1963; Hippisley Coxe, 1973; Houghton, 2000; BBC, 2014; Johnson, 2017.

## Sir John Schorne

Area: North Marston

Date: 1290–1314

There is some debate whether it was a boot or a drinking horn, but all the images seem to indicate that it is a long boot, as was the style of the period. The local rhyme at the start of the story seems to back this up, and if you exchange boot for horn the whole piece rhymes. However, the popular image that is shown, and was even part of the stained-glass image of the church, is a boot; this lends weight to the belief that the story grew from the saying 'beating down Satan under his foot', which in practice meant being so devout as to self-mortify. In this case, John Shorne had the devil 'under his boot', meaning he had overcome temptation and sin. This is backed by contemporary reports of John being pious. The story is well known, but there is scant information; in most cases only saying John Shorne conjured the devil into a boot. Therefore, I have had to use some artistic license in order to develop the story for this collection.

Although the well is now inaccessible, it was once so wide that people could bathe in it as well as drink from it.

Sources: *The Bucks Free Press*, 1882; Uttley, 1950; Archer, 1989; Lucas, 1993; Houghton, 1996, 2000; Westwood and Simpson, 2005.

## The Bard in Bernwood

Area: Grendon Underwood

Date: Turn of seventeenth century

Buckinghamshire has another Shakespearian link, as Stony Stratford is the only Stratford to be mentioned in any of Shakespeare's plays. It appears in *Richard III* Act 2 scene IV as the place where the young King Edward V is staying before his abduction by his villainous uncle Richard Duke of Gloucester, later King Richard III.

Sources: *The Bucks Free Press*, 1882; Uttley, 1950; Archer, 1989.

### Niel Shortshirt

Area: Brill

Date: Pre-1066

Niel is also sometimes Nigel (a name that wouldn't have been in Britain until after the Norman Conquest). In 1266, Henry III believed the story, and confirmed it as true when he granted the area anew to the Fitzniels/Fitznigels, the ancestors of Niel/Nigel the boar slayer. The castle at Boarstall was pulled down by Sir John Aubrey in the late 1600s after his five-year-old son was accidently poisoned and died. Sir John left the house as he could not bear to live there, but soon even the thought of it still standing was too much, and so it was pulled down.

During the Civil War both Boarstall and Brill were important strongholds: Brill was held by the Parliamentarians and Boarstall by the Royalists. Princess Elizabeth (daughter of Henry VIII) was held at Boarstall when Queen Mary held the throne; she was worried about Elizabeth's claim to the throne. Elizabeth had many supporters: Mary had reverted to Catholicism and many Protestants wanted Elizabeth as Queen because she would restore the Church of England. When Queen Mary (Elizabeth's older half-sister) sent for Elizabeth, Elizabeth knew she was in trouble and probably facing imprisonment in the Tower of London, or even execution, so she escaped through the moated passage, disguised as a dairymaid.

In the north of the county there is another horn, the Purlieu Horn (1692), which was the charter given to the Dayrell family granting them hunting rights as the ranger of the Whittlewood Forest.

There is also a story from Chetwood, which bares remarkable resemblance to the Niel Shortshirt tale, including the monstrous boar and granting of rights of land and tithes by the charter of a horn (and gathered by lads from the surrounding villages of Finmere and Tingewick, where the lads would be given gingerbread and beer). A farmer in 1810 near Chetwood decided to remove a large mound from his field and in it he discovered a huge skeleton of a boar.

Source: *The Bucks Free Press*, 1882; Uttley, 1950; Westwood and Simpson, 2005.

## *The Soulbury Stone*

Area: Soulbury

Date: Various

The Soulbury Stone is actually a glacial erratic, carried from Derbyshire (the place of its origin) to its current position by a glacier during the last ice age. In that sense, the stone journeyed to Soulbury by natural forces, without the aid of man. This is an example of how sometimes folk tales can be closer to the truth than is expected.

Sources: *The Bucks Free Press*, 1882; Archer, 1989; Houghton, 1994; Westwood and Simpson, 2005; Addley, 2016.

## *A Ghostly Guard Dog*

Area: Soulbury

Date: Various

This is a most unusual story of a good-natured ghost dog; however, there have also been ghostly encounters throughout the county of pet pooches coming back to warn their masters of trouble.

Sources: Houghton, 1994; Westwood and Simpson, 2005; Addley, 2016.

## The Black Dog

Area: Aylesbury

Date: Pre-twentieth century

This dog seems to utterly fit the profile of terrifying hounds from hell, which seem to be protecting something – whether it is territory or treasure we shall never know. Throughout the county there have been sightings of another elusive beast: the Buckinghamshire Beast – a black-furred creature supposedly of enormous size, and considered to be either a black panther or a leopard. Every few years there seems to a recurrence of sightings, so keep your eyes peeled!

Sources: Hartland, 2000; Topham, 2015.

## St Rumbold

Area: Buckingham

Date: AD 650

Sometimes Rumbold is confused with the Irish Saint Rumbold of Mechelen, who lived to adulthood and become a missionary. The St Rumbold in the story is sometimes cited as St Rumwold, but the most common version of his name in current use is Rumbold. Rumbold is not the only heavenly visitor to Buckingham. There is an account of a three-year-old in Buckinghamshire having been burnt whilst his mother had briefly stepped out of the house to attend to the livestock. As he lay dying with his mother by his side, he reportedly saw a heavenly angelic man in the room, who was waiting for him.

Sources: Historic England, n.d.; Shirley, n.d.; *The Bucks Free Press*, 1882; Heath, 1912; Briggs, 1991; Lucas, 1993; Houghton, 1996; Kidd-Hewitt, 2008.

## The Centaur

Area: Quarrendon

Date: 1988

This is a most curious case, there doesn't seem to have been anything else like it locally. David Kidd-Hewitt, who is a researcher renowned for his knowledge of ghost stories, found that there was a possible explanation for it. He suggests that, as the field was the site of a Civil War battle, it may indeed be the ghost of a cavalryman slumped over his horse. However, this doesn't match the description of the witnesses who say they saw the torso.

Sources: Uttley, 1950; Kidd-Hewitt, 2008.

## The Last Message

Area: Haddenham

Date: 1830s

In and around the same time, a number of gruesome murders took place both within Buckinghamshire and its neighbouring counties; some of them even included a family member, usually a wife, witnessing the attack through a ghostly vision. It is no wonder that a good story such as this travels, especially one attached to a traumatic experience or some supernatural phenomenon. This story has a number of well-recounted sources taken from, or within a generation of, the event.

Sources: Harman, 1934; Hippisley Coxe, 1973; Archer, 1987; Briggs, 1991; Matthews, 2004; Westwood and Simpson, 2005.

# STORIES FROM MILTON KEYNES

## *From-Crete Cows and Roundabouts*

Area: Milton Keynes

Dates: 1967

Milton Keynes often has a bad reputation with those who live outside its borders, but those who know it well often herald its landscaped design, parklands, and its mix of old and new. It has also, in a very short period of time, developed many urban myths to complement the histories and folk tales that emanate from its many older parts such as Bletchley, Milton Keynes Village, Wolverton and Stony Stratford. Strictly speaking, urban myths may feel a bit modern in a book on folk tales; however, what are urban myths if not the folk tales of tomorrow?

Sources: Kitchen, 2014, 2018; word of mouth.

## *The Guardian*

Area: Milton Keynes Village and Woughton-on-the-Green

Date: Turn of twentieth century

This tale was recounted to Mr H. Harman in the Old Swan in Woughton on the Green. Harman had engaged the locals with discussions about local ghost stories, most notably Old Curly, who is said to haunt Curly's Bush with his dog, appearing to terrify any poor soul who happens to be passing that way late at night. The locals in the pub scoffed, saying that whilst their father's generation had believed in such things, they knew of no one who had seen Curly, or even believed in it anymore. The discussion then proceeded to other stories, including this one told by one of the brothers who appears in the story. He claimed the event happened to him; the rest of the locals listened attentively, and no one disputed the tale once it had ended.

Sources: Harman, 1934.

*Heart of Treason!*
Area: Newport Pagnell
Date: 1605
Sir Everard Digby was only twenty-five at the time of the Gunpowder Plot. His ghost is said to haunt Digby Walk – the escape path that led down to a spring that was famous in Roman times. It was here Digby hid when the authorities first came looking for him.

A few years before the Gunpowder Plot, Gayhurst had been under suspicion for harbouring Catholics. There was a secret room in the house created by a false ceiling. This was discovered by investigators, who lit every room in the house. When they could see one window that was not lit, they knew there was a secret room and that a Catholic priest had been hidden there. This caused the Digbys to be closely monitored.

It is said the snails at Gayhurst are descendants of French edible snails that escaped.
Sources: *The Bucks Free Press*, 1882; Uttley, 1950; Archer, 1989; Houghton, 1993, 1994.

*The Stony Gunpowder Plot*
Area: Stony Stratford
Date: 1859
This story was a delight for a storyteller to discover about her own town. It is simple, but perhaps that is why it is one of my favourite tales.
Sources: Dunleavy, 2019.

*Mischievous Monks*
Area: Newport Pagnell
Date: 1275–1340
This story completely smashes the saintly image of most monks. These Bad Boys of the Bible seemed hell-bent on

partying, rioting and doing as they darn well please. It is no wonder, then, that given a couple of hundred years the Hellfire Club should appear in the same county. I believe Simon de Rede would have approved of Sir Francis.

Sources: Houghton, 1996.

### The Devil's House

Area: Olney

Date: Unknown

It was said that the devil only showed himself to those who wanted to see him, which does suggest the people of Olney were once rather naughtier than the pretty town now might indicate.

Olney's Pancake Race also has an international link-up with the women of Liberal, Kansas USA. All racers have to wear the headscarf and apron like in the 1445 story and be residents of Olney, but they occasionally let outsiders run after the main event in a mini race. In 2016 I ran the Pancake Race in full Restoration dress and wig to celebrate the re-opening of the Cowper Newton Museum. [Note from Stephen Hobbs: 'Ay, you were across that road like a whippet!']

Sources: *The Bucks Free Press*, 1882; Ratcliff, 1907; Uttley, 1950; Lucas, 1993; Houghton, 1994; Kidd-Hewitt, 2008; Topham, 2015.

### A Cock and Bull Story

Area: Stony Stratford

Date: Various

Stony Stratford residents will happily inform everyone that the town is the true origin of the phrase, although they themselves take this with more than a pinch of salt. It even appears in *Brewer's Dictionary*. Yet the term goes back much further than the name of the two taverns that stand just metres apart on Stony Stratford High Street. Some say it comes from Aesop's fables, where talking animals highlight our moral (or lack of) guidelines; others say it comes from the French 'coq a lane', which also developed the Scottish 'cock a layne'. It appears in Robert Burton's medical text on depression (1621), and John Day – a contemporary of Shakespeare – used it in *Law-trickes or Who Would have thought it*, a comedy in 1608: 'what a tale of a cock and bull he told my father'. Or it might just be a shortened version of a 'concocted and bully story'. Whatever its origin, the term cock and bull means made up and fanciful, so in that sense the tale of Stony Stratford as the origin of the term is a total cock and bull story.

Sources: Room, 2001; word of mouth.

## Bread, Beer and Beef!

Area: Wolverton

Date: 1838

A story about Wolverton just had to include its famous railway history, which quite literally built the town, for Wolverton was the new town before the 'new town' (Milton Keynes) existed. Bryan Dunleavy, upon whose website this story was found, is a master historian of local knowledge, and although he no longer lives in the area he continues to write books and collect many stories about Wolverton and neighbouring Stony Stratford. It is with the greatest respect that I turn to his work for inspiration.

Sources: Dunleavy, 2019.

## The Grave Robbers

Area: Stony Stratford

Date: Nineteenth century

Grave robbery had become such an issue during the nineteenth century that laws were changed to allow the medical profession to use real bodies for medical science; before this it was thought unholy to open up the dead. Although the bodies used were usually the bodies of executed convicts, there were not enough of these bodies to go around, and so medical practitioners would often pay large sums of money (and ask no questions) in order to get extra bodies for dissection. Therefore, whether for medical cash or plunder, grave robbery became popular with felons.

Sources: Cargill and Fuller, 1994; Ewart Barley, 2003.

## The Witch of Horsefair Green

Area: Stony Stratford

Date: Pre-eighteenth century

The houses on Horsefair Green are no longer thatched and it is hard to tell which is the house discussed in the story, although the most likely cottage is on the last bit of the green that connects to Silver Street. Next to it was a pub in days gone by and there are images of both the pub and the tiny cottage with thatched roofs.

Sources: Cargill and Fuller, 1994; Ewart Barley, 2003.

## Polly Parrot

Area: New Bradwell

Date: Around 1909

Living Archive is a wonderful organisation that over the years has recorded the personal stories of the residents and builders of Milton Keynes, adding a wonderful resource to the heritage of the new town. Along with the documented planning of the area, and the histories from the older parts of Milton Keynes, it is hoped the folk tales here will provide a more inclusive insight of this new, old town.

Sources: Mundy, 1992.

## Dick Turpin

Area: Woughton-on-the-Green and Stony Stratford

Date: 1730s

Although Dick Turpin was active as a highwayman during the 1730s, the romantic accounts of his fictional adventures begin about a hundred years later when writer William Harrison Ainsworth wrote about Dick Turpin and Black Bess (an invented equine sidekick). He tells of Dick riding Black Bess like the wind through the night from London to York (a 200-mile journey) to escape a crime and to achieve an alibi in York. These romantic tales became very popular during the Victorian times and many places developed their own Dick Turpin stories, often elaborated from other local highwaymen stories. For instance, Claude Duvall was the icon of romantic highwaymen with much charm and grace; although he operated in the mid-1600s, a number of his stories were adapted to become the more famous Dick Turpin.

Sources: *The Bucks Free Press*, 1882; Harman, 1934; Uttley, 1950; Hippisley Coxe, 1973; Houghton, 1995, 1996; Matthews, 2004; Westwood and Simpson, 2005; Dunleavy, Daniels and Powell, 2014; Topham, 2015; word of mouth.

## Tally Ho! Hanmer

Area: Simpson

Date: Unknown (sometime between 1773–1830)

Such a brief note of a story held such potential, for there seems nothing more enjoyable than when someone who should behave starts to bend, break, and bulldoze the rules. Tally Ho! seems to be a cad on the people's side.

Sources: Fowler, 1892; Page, 1927; Legg, 1991; Houghton, 1994.

## Penny a Peek

Area: Stony Stratford

Date: Unknown

I happened to find this story in the run up to Halloween in 2017. I was walking down the High Street in Stony Stratford to see the shop windows decorated with numerous skeletons and couldn't help remark to my companion that the tradition of hanging up bodies in Stony Stratford was still alive and kicking, unlike the bodies.

Sources: Cargill and Fuller, 1994; Houghton, 1996.

## The Tallest Spire in Bucks

Area: Hanslope

Date: 1730s

Robert Cadman not only fixed roofs but became famed for being a 'ropeslider', walking great lengths of rope stretched between buildings or over rivers, or pinned from the ground to the highest point of a nearby building. He died in 1739 when a rope he was walking on snapped.

In 1804, the Hanslope church spire was hit by lightning (so the spire you see now is not the one fixed by Robert) and had to be rebuilt. When it was reconstructed it was made shorter, now only measuring 186 feet (57 metres), but it is still the tallest spire in Buckinghamshire.

Sources: *The Bucks Free Press*, 1882; Uttley, 1950; Houghton, 1994.

## Madame Bennett

Area: Calverton and Galley Hill

Date: 1694

There is some ambiguity as to when the murder happened: in 1693, 1694, or before. One version says the niece was in the house, and another that she was visiting and found her aunt. Some versions say it was three men, some point the

finger at Adam Barnes, and a connection to a field called Roger's Grave where the murderer was supposed to be buried. The most common form of the tale is presented here.
Sources: *The Bucks Free Press*, 1882; Archer, 1989; Cargill and Fuller, 1994; Ewart Barley, 2003; Westwood and Simpson, 2005.

## The Fenny Forger
Area: Fenny Stratford
Date: Roman

For this story I had to use a lot of artistic license, but from the moment I found the reference to a hoard of money forging equipment from Roman times it lit up my imagination, thinking of all the ways this could come about.
Sources: Houghton, 1996.

## The Shooting Party
Area: Bletchley
Date: 1938

There is now a pub in Bletchley called Captain Ridley's Shooting Party (formerly the Bletchley Arms).

The story of Bletchley Park is a fascinating one; it consists of thousands of stories created by the men and women who worked around the clock (in shifts lasting eight hours or more in fourteen-day stints) in huts that were freezing cold during the winters and baking hot in the summers. Although most of them did not know it (so strict was the secrecy even between huts), they were working to crack the German Enigma machine codes in order to decipher the encrypted messages of German troops. The brightest and best of British intelligence, university students, and debutante society were ordered to report to Station X at Bletchley Park. Among them, Alan Turing led a small team to create Colossus – the first modern computer. Alan was considered quite a humorous and eccentric fellow who used to cycle to work wearing his gas mask during the spring and summer, as he suffered terribly from hay fever – or so the urban myths tell us.

People who worked there have since broken their silence, telling us many things about the everyday life at the park that most say resembled more of a university campus atmosphere than what you might expect from a covert intelligence operation. They say the tea was terrible and, on occasion, so the fable says, people would even find cockroaches in their food. And all the time they were harbouring the biggest secret of the twentieth century – a remarkable feat considering that some 10,000 people worked there. Those men and women kept their silence for thirty years. Bletchley Park museum has done remarkable work in tracking down many of the workers and piecing together a picture of the true story of Bletchley Park.

Sources: Bletchley Park, n.d.; McKay, 2011.

## Stories from the Stony Storytellers

### *A Lacemaker or Lucky Gemma*
Area: Stony Stratford
Date: 1800s
Lynette says:

> I created Lucky Gemma for the 2019 Bard of Stony Stratford Trials, which required the performance of three original pieces. I wanted to include lacemaking in one of my stories because it was such an important and little remembered part of Stony Stratford history. I like the fact that, while difficult work, it gave a respectable woman an honourable way to create an independent income. I was also struck by the fact that Victorian do-gooders and others

believed that they could keep young girls off the path to immorality by getting them involved in the lacemaking trade. And from that, through the magic of the creative process, which I can't really explain, came the character of Gemma and her story.

Sources: Lynette Hill; Cowper and Newton Museum,n.d.; MK Heritage, no date; Barlett, 1991; Makovicky, Hopkin and Dame Evans, 2018.

## Curly Kale and Quinoa
Area: Stony Stratford
Date: Unknown

Phil Chippendale was the fourth Bard of Stony Stratford. He began as a storyteller in 2015 and was often noted for his improvised comic style. During his Bardic year, he developed poetry and created some notable stories.

Sources: Phil Chippendale.

## Jim and Mabel
Area: Stony Stratford
Date: 1920s

Stephen says:

> I was told this story by Jim and Mabel's daughter in 2017, and though I noted its bare bones in five short sentences, I then forgot all about it! I only remembered it when Terrie challenged us (the Stony Storytellers) in 2018 to find or create a folk tale featuring a familiar place. At the time, a street mural was being painted of Queen Eleanor in Stony Stratford and I began to think about people who weren't being honoured in such a tangible way. And this is how 'Jim and Mabel' began. Their daughter (she chooses to remain anonymous) subsequently gave me many more details,

and my story is true to the original. I added the authentic details about the Rendezvous tram (its capacity was actually 120), and the story of the two old men trying to cross the street is probably apocryphal and comes from any town with a very busy high street. 'Jim and Mabel' remained an oral story until Terrie requested a written version for this book in 2019.

Sources: Word of mouth; Stephen Hobbs.

*Once Upon a Milton Keynes*

Area: Milton Keynes

Date: 2017

This story was created as part of PhD research, and I wanted to create a modern folk tale as a summary of the research itself. It focuses on the poor image Milton Keynes has, how this affects its residents, and how through stories this image can be 're-storyed' or redefined in order to create a more positive reputation for the area and a stronger sense of place for its residents.

Sources: Terrie Howey.

# BIBLIOGRAPHY

## BOOKS

Archer, J. (1987) *Tales of Old Buckinghamshire* (Newbury: Countryside).

Archer, J. (1989) *Hidden Buckinghamshire* (Newbury: Countryside).

Bartlett, L. (1991) *Lace Villages* (Cambridge: B.T. Batsford).

Briggs, K.M. (1991) *A Dictionary of British Folk-Tales Incorporating the F.J. Norton Collection: Part B (Vols 1 & 2) Folk Legends.* (London: Routledge).

Cargill, J. and Fuller, N. (1994) *The Time Walk: a tour through the history and folklore of Stony Stratford, Passenham and Calverton* (J. Cargill & N. Fuller).

Dunleavy, B., Daniels, K. and Powell, A. (2014) *Inns of Stony Stratford* (Southampton: Magic Flute).

Ewart Barley, R. (2003) *Romance Around Stony Stratford*, 2nd edn (Leicester: Syston).

Fowler, J.K. (1892) *Echoes of Old Country Life: Being Recollections of Sport, Politics, and Farming in the Good Old Times* (London: E. Arnold).

Fowler, J.K. (1894) *Recollections of Old Country Life, Social, Political, Sporting & Agricultural* (London: Longmans).

Hallam, J. (1972) *The Haunted Inns of England* (London: Wolfe).

Harman, H. (1934) *Sketches to the Bucks Countryside* (London: Blandford).

Hartland, E.S. (2000) *English Fairy and Folk Tales* (New York: Dover).

Hippisley Coxe, A.D. (1973) *Haunted Britain* (London: Hutchinson & Co.).

Houghton, J. (1993) *Murders and Mysteries, People and Plots* (Dunstable: The Book Castle).

Houghton, J. (1994) *Eccentrics & Villains, Hauntings & Heroes* (Dunstable: The Book Castle).

Houghton, J. (1995) *Myth & Witches, Puzzles & Politics* (Dunstable: The Book Castle).

Houghton, J. (1996) *Manors & Mayhem, Paupers & Parsons* (Dunstable: The Book Castle).

Houghton, J. (2000) *Sanctity & Scandal in Bedfordshire & Buckingham* (Dunstable: The Book Castle).

Kidd-Hewitt, D. (2008) *Buckinghamshire: Stories of the Supernatural* (Newbury: Countryside).

Kitchen, R. (2014) *Milton Keynes Through the Lens* (England: Living Archive).

Kitchen, R. (2018) *Make No little Plans* (England: Living Archive).

Lucas, J. (1993) *Buckinghamshire Curiosities: A Guide to Follies and Strange Buildings, Curious Tales and Unusual People* (Wimbourne: Dovecote).

Matthews, R. (2004) *Haunted Places of Bedfordshire and Buckinghamshire* (Newbury: Countryside).

McKay, S. (2011) *The Secret Life of Bletchley Park* (London: Aurum).

Mundy, H. (1992) *I'll Tell You What Happened …* (Milton Keynes: Living Archive).

Page, W. (1927) *A History of the County of Buckingham: Vol*

*IV* (London: Victoria County History).

Piper, K. (1996) *To Pass the Music On: Songs and Rhymes from Buckinghamshire* (Buckingham: Northward).

Room, A. (2001) *Brewer's Dictionary of Phrase and Fable* (London: Cassell & Co).

Tongue, R,L. (1970) *Forgotten Folk-tales of the English Counties* (London: Routledge).

Uttley, A. (1950) *Buckinghamshire* (London: Robert Hale).

Westwood, J. and Simpson, J. (2005) *The Lore of the Land: A Guide to England's Legends, from Spring-Heeled Jack to the Witches of Warboys* (London: Penguin Books).

Woodley, L. (2009) *Murderous Intent: A Collection of Murders in Buckinghamshire* (Copt Hewick: Book Castle).

## WEBSITES/ARTICLES ONLINE

Addley, E. (2016) 'The Soulbury stone never loses – and now the council knows it', *The Guardian*. Available at: www.theguardian.com/science/2016/apr/02/the-soulbury-stone-never-loses-and-now-the-council-knows-it (Accessed: 28 November 2018).

Amersham musuem (2016) 'Amersham Martyrs', *Amersham Museum*. Available at: amershammuseum.org/history/research/religion/martyrs (Accessed: 1 February 2019).

BBC (2014) The Passion: Judas, *BBC*. Available at: www.bbc.co.uk/thepassion/articles/joseph_of_arimathea.shtml (Accessed: 1 February 2019).

Bletchley Park (n.d) *Our Story, Bletchley Park*. Available at: bletchleypark.org.uk/our-story (Accessed: 20 February 2019).

Bucks Free Press and Andrews-Reading, M. (2004) 'Martyrs died after row with church', *Bucks Free Press*. Available at: www.bucksfreepress.co.uk/news/535506.

martyrs-died-after-row-with-church (Accessed: 1 February 2019).

Cowper and Newton Museum (n.d). Available at: www.cowperandnewtonmuseum.org.uk/lace-making/

Dancer, L. (2016) 'In Pictures: South Bucks' most haunted', *Bucks Free Press*. Available at: www.bucksfreepress.co.uk/news/14431351.in-pictures-south-bucks-most-haunted (Accessed: 28 November 2018).

Deloney, T. (1632) *Thomas of Reading, Thomas Deloney: His Thomas of Reading: And Three Ballads on the Spanish Armada*. Available at: archive.org/details/thomasdeloney-hi00delogoog/page/n26 (Accessed: 21 February 2019).

Dunleavy, B. (2019) *Wolverton Past – History before 1970*. Available at: wolvertonpast.blogspot.com (Accessed: 20 October 2018).

Editors of Encyclopaedia Britannica (2019) *Claude Duval, Encyclopaedia Britannica*. Available at: www.britannica.com/biography/Claude-Duval (Accessed: 21 February 2019).

Geocaching (2003) 'Geocaching – The Official Global GPS Cache Hunt Site'. Available at: www.geocaching.com/geocache/GCGGC9_the-witches-stone-bucks?guid=e0bb1b2f-022d-407a-88a6-f991745412a7 (Accessed: 30 January 2019).

George, S. (2018) 'Older than Dracula: in search of the English vampire', *The Conversation*. Available at: theconversation.com/older-than-dracula-in-search-of-the-english-vampire-105238 (Accessed: 30 January 2019).

Heath, S. (1912) 'Pilgrim Life in the Middle Ages'. Available at: https://books.google.com/books?id=qqYMAAAAIAAJ&pg=PA227&lpg=PA227&dq=rood+of+grace#v=onepage&q=rood of grace&f=false (Accessed: 29 January 2019).

Historic England (n.d) *St Rumbold's Well, Buckingham – 1017204, Historic England*. Historic England. Available at: historicengland.org.uk/listing/the-list/list-entry/1017204 (Accessed: 29 January 2019).

Johnson, B. (2017) *Give Us Our Eleven Days, The English Calendar Riots of 1752, Historic UK*. Available at: www.historic-uk.com/HistoryUK/HistoryofBritain/Give-us-our-eleven-days (Accessed: 1 February 2019).

Legg, E. (1991) 'Buckinghamshire returns of the census of religious worship, 1851'. Buckinghamshire Record Society. Available at: www.genuki.org.uk/big/eng/BKM/Simpson (Accessed: 8 February 2019).

Makovicky, N., Hopkin, D. and Dame Evans, J. (2018) 'A lacemaker's home in Milton Keynes. The reminiscences of Dame Joan Evans', *By the Poor, for the Rich: Lace in Context*. Available at: laceincontext.com/a-lacemakers-home-in-milton-keynes-the-reminiscences-of-dame-joan-evans (Accessed: 19 February 2019).

MK Heritage (n.d) 'Stony Stratford: Lacing Making in Stony Stratford'. Available at: www.mkheritage.co.uk/mkm/stonystratford/docs/lace.html (Accessed: 19 February 2019).

Occult-Media (2018) 'Buckinghamshire Vampire – Occult World'. Available at: occult-world.com/famous-vampires/buckinghamshire-vampire (Accessed: 30 January 2019).

Ratcliff, O. (1907) 'Part 1 of 3, Oliver Ratcliff's "Olney, Bucks"', in *Olney Almanack*. Available at: www.mkheritage.org.uk/odhs-files/pdfs/Olney Bucks 1907 Part 1a.pdf (Accessed: 21 February 2019).

Shenley Church End Parish Council (n.d.) *History*. Available at: www.shenleychurchend-pc.co.uk/page28.html (Accessed: 1 February 2019).

Shirley, R. (n.d.) St *Rumbold of Buckingham*, *The University of Buckingham*. Available at: www.buckingham.ac.uk/about/history/rumbold (Accessed: 29 January 2019).

Smith, E. (2018) 'History of Watches, Development of Wristwatches', *On Time, Govberg*. Available at: www.govbergwatches.com/blog/history-of-horology (Accessed: 19 February 2019).

The Bucks Free Press (1882) 'Buckinghamshire Curiosities of Local History'.

The Gentleman's Magazine archives (n.d.) *The Gentleman's Magazine.* Available at: onlinebooks.library. upenn.edu/webbin/serial?id=gentlemans (Accessed: 29 November 2018).

Topham, I. (2012) 'Buckinghamshire Revenant',*Mysterious Britain & Ireland.* Available at: www.mysteriousbritain. co.uk/wp/uncategorized/buckinghamshire-revenant (Accessed: 29 November 2018).

Topham, I. (2015) 'A gazetteer of folklore, myths and legends and the paranormal', *Mysterious Britain & Ireland.* Available at: www.mysteriousbritain.co.uk (Accessed: 19 February 2018).

*Wolverton Express* (1963) 'Miracle Thorn'.

**Society** *for*
**Storytelling**

Since 1993, The Society for Storytelling has championed the ancient art of oral storytelling and its long and honourable history – not just as entertainment, but also in education, health, and inspiring and changing lives. Storytellers, enthusiasts and academics support and are supported by this registered charity to ensure the art is nurtured and developed throughout the UK.

Many activities of the Society are available to all, such as locating storytellers on the Society website, taking part in our annual National Storytelling Week at the start of every February, purchasing our quarterly magazine Storylines, or attending our Annual Gathering – a chance to revel in engaging performances, inspiring workshops, and the company of like-minded people.

You can also become a member of the Society to support the work we do. In return, you receive free access to Storylines, discounted tickets to the Annual Gathering and other storytelling events, the opportunity to join our mentorship scheme for new storytellers, and more. Among our great deals for members is a 30% discount off titles from The History Press.

For more information, including how to join, please visit

www.sfs.org.uk